ALSO BY JAMES VAN SWEDEN

Gardening with Water

Bold Romantic Gardens (with Wolfgang Oehme
and Susan Rademacher Frey)

GARDENING
WITH
NATURE

Gardening
with
Nature

James van Sweden

Random House 🏠 New York

WARNING

All do-it-yourself activities involve a degree of risk. Skills, materials, tools, and site conditions vary widely. Although the author has made every effort to ensure accuracy, the reader remains responsible for the selection and use of tools, materials, and methods. Always obey local codes and laws, follow manufacturers' operating instructions, and observe safety precautions.

Copyright © 1997 by Oehme, van Sweden & Associates, Inc.

All rights reserved under International and Pan-American Copyright Conventions. Published in the United States by Random House, Inc., New York, and simultaneously in Canada by Random House of Canada Limited, Toronto.

The photographs on pages iii, iv, v, xii, 1 and 22 are by Roger Foley.
Page viii: Hans Hofmann, *Bird Cage—Variation II*. Courtesy of André Emmerich Gallery.
The photographs on pages x and xvi are by Richard Felber.
The photograph on page xv is by Jerry Harpur.

Library of Congress Cataloging-in-Publication Data
van Sweden, James
Gardening with nature: How James van Sweden and Wolfgang Oehme plant
slopes, meadows, outdoor rooms, and garden screens/James van Sweden.
p. cm.
Includes index.
ISBN 0-679-42947-6
1. Natural gardens, American. 2. Gardens—United States.
I. Oehme, Wolfgang. II. Title.
SB457.53.V35 1997
712—dc21 97-5145

Random House website address: http://www.randomhouse.com/

Printed in the Singapore on acid-free paper
24689753
First Edition

DESIGNED BY JOEL AVIROM & JASON SNYDER

To the memory of
Roberto Burle Marx

"*We can combine so many plants together that we can
think they are doing erotic color movements.*"

—R.B.M.

ACKNOWLEDGMENTS

My twenty-seven-year partnership with Wolfgang Oehme has been successful, productive, and pleasurable beyond our wildest dreams. Design collaboration between strong personalities can at times be trying, but we have been able to overcome our difficulties with humor and honest exchanges of ideas. Wolfgang and I approach landscape architecture from different backgrounds; mine is in architecture and his, horticulture. For us, this has been a magical combination.

Helen Pratt, my literary agent, believed in this series from the beginning. She introduced me to Random House and to my editor, Jason Epstein, who brilliantly set the book's voice and style. Both have become good and supportive friends in the process. I am also grateful to Joy de Menil, Walter Weintz, Martha Schwartz, Kathy Rosenbloom, and Joanne Barracca.

Robin Herbst was invaluable as a reader, applying her deftly critical eye and sharp pencil. Joel Avirom designed this beautiful book while patiently allowing me to look over his shoulder. Photographers Richard Felber and Roger Foley captured our vision on film.

Wolfgang and I enjoy collaborations with other professionals. The landscape architects and architects who participated in the design of many of the gardens described in the "Portfolio of Gardens" include Stephen Carr, Elissa Cullman, Nancy Watkins Denig, Elliott Rosenblum, Mark Simon, Suman Sorg, and Bernard Wharton. Also, Dr. Frank Gouin shared his vast knowledge of ornamental horticulture, especially concerning soil conditions. Generous assistance was given by Barbara Bolling Woodward, Martha Turner, Dr. H. Marc Cathey, Darrel G. Morrison, Conrad Hamerman, A. E. Bye, Karyl Jo Mangus, and Johanna van Sweden.

A work of this magnitude could not be realized without the dedication and sacrifice of our professional staff. Charles E. Turner skillfully wrote and edited the text with me. Project landscape architects Sandra Youssef Clinton, Eric D. Groft, and Sheila A. Brady developed the garden designs with Wolfgang and me and supervised their construction. They were supported by H. Paul Davis, Patricia McManus, Bob Hruby, and Ariel Gelman. Jeffrey A. Charlesworth, Ching-Fang Chen, and Susanne Fyffe made the beautiful pencil drawings. Raymond E. Nuesch researched and drafted Part IV, "Favorite Plants," with Wolfgang. Barbara C. Rho provided word-processing and clerical assistance. Marcia K. Oresky kept accurate accounts.

Finally, I want to thank the garden owners for permitting us to photograph their gardens and for taking time to be interviewed. Their candid comments add important personal touches to the garden descriptions. Our daring clients make it possible for Wolfgang and me to build our fantasies.

CONTENTS

INTRODUCTION

My hope is that *Gardening with Nature* will inspire you to bring nature's full bounty into your gardening life. I want to entice you to create a garden that is in harmony with nature, regardless of its size; a garden that celebrates seasonal change and is easy to maintain. I also want to teach you something of what I have learned, so that after reading this, you will never look at a garden in the same way again.

This book, the second in a series about garden design, addresses the practical and aesthetic values of plants. My objective is not to give you an easy formula for building a garden but to show you the guiding principles that Wolfgang Oehme and I have arrived at over the course of our long and fruitful partnership. Since each of us looks at gardens differently, I hope you will review the principles and ideas in these pages, study the photographs and drawings, go out and do some field research, and then follow your own instincts. A few words of advice before we depart: above all, don't take it too seriously, and have a wonderful time along the way.

Two fundamental principles guide our efforts. The first is our appreciation for plants—for their intrinsic beauty and for their particular, idiosyncratic growth habits. The other is careful regard for garden composition, and especially the proper placement of plants. With these two principles in mind we test a garden's success by viewing it from different angles. From a bench or path in the midst of a garden we enjoy the touch and fragrance of plants. Outside—from the street or a building—we regard the garden like a stage set that changes from act to act with the seasons. From a greater distance the garden takes on the appearance of a vast work of art—a collage or painting—spread across the ground plane. These are the elements that make garden building an art form.

To create any work of art it is important to understand composition and harmony as well as to know your raw materials. But garden building also requires an appreciation for the ephemeral nature of plants: gardens are alive; they grow and become more beautiful over time, even if left alone.

Like many gardeners, I find special pleasure in studying garden history and tradition. Whenever I travel I look for gardens to photograph and sketch. Studying as many gardens as possible helps me to understand which combinations of colors and juxtapositions of forms are most pleasing. I draw on these impressions, often subconsciously, when I design. But my own small garden in the center of Washington, D.C., just seventeen feet wide and fifty-five feet deep, is one of my greatest learning tools. For more than twenty-five years it has been a tiny laboratory where I try out new plants for form and color. I study their changes from season to season and year to year from my kitchen table. This has resulted in minor adjustments over the years, but the basic design that Wolfgang and I developed in 1971 has not changed. Wolfgang uses his half-acre garden in suburban Baltimore to test both individual plant species and unusual combinations. It too has been a valuable learning tool. Wolfgang scrutinizes his plants for boldness of form and texture, and for their hardiness. He looks for plants that are natural and relaxed, with beautiful flowers in strong colors.

Over the years, Wolfgang and I have applied what we have learned in our own gardens to our many commissioned projects. We use the same principles for small and large gardens; size is not important. Gardening is a rewarding challenge at every scale. Success results when gardens are both bold and romantic and—most important of all—peaceful to the gardener's eye.

The foundation of this book is our personal vision. My hope is to describe this vision and to challenge you to pursue your instincts. Build your skills step-by-step, and soon you will reap rewards in your own garden.

Using This Book

Part I, "Evolution of a Style," describes the forces that set my career with Wolfgang Oehme in motion, as well as how we came to invent the "New American Garden" style. In the "Influences" chapter, I highlight early formative experiences and describe events and influences that led to our partnership in 1975. This chapter also introduces other designers from America and abroad whose gardens inspire us.

By the late 1970s, Wolfgang and I had been credited with a whole new approach to American gardening. This approach, frequently called the New American Garden style, is the subject of a brief chapter that describes our personal vision of gardening and the underlying philosophy that supports it.

Part II, "Planting Our Gardens," summarizes how we go about designing and building our gardens. In "Elements of Design," I describe the step-by-step process, from our first meeting with a client to the preparation of a final plan. Then I follow the completed garden through the seasons, describing what makes it successful over the years. "Portfolio of Gardens" is a "tour" that includes every scale of garden—from a planted terrace high above the streets of Manhattan to suburban gardens and rolling rural estates. Short essays, complemented by photographs and drawings, describe each garden's geographical context, its inherent problems and opportunities, and our design responses.

Part III, "Planting Your Garden Step-by-Step," moves beyond our professional achievements to show how you can create your own beautiful and personally satisfying garden. "Start with a Base Drawing" describes the drawing you will need, how to prepare it, and what information it should include. In a chapter called "Evaluate Your Property," I recommend a process that starts with a fresh look at your garden space and ends with recommendations on how to test your soil. In "Create a Planting Scheme," I offer some helpful advice on garden design and outline a sequence of tasks that will help you develop your own planting scheme. Once you have a planting scheme, you are ready to proceed with building the garden; "Prepare and Plant Your Garden" is a hands-on guide that tells you everything you need to know, from flagging utility lines to spreading the final topdressing of mulch. And finally, in "Establish and Maintain Your Garden," I share some secrets I have learned over the years for keeping your garden in great shape.

Part IV, "Favorite Plants," offers a short, descriptive list of our all-time favorite plants. The list is accompanied by photographs and drawings that show many of these plants in a garden setting. Throughout the book, I have identified plants by their botanical names. Botanical names ensure accuracy since common names vary from place to place. I have added common names in parentheses after botanical names only for plants that are not included in the "Favorite Plants" listing. When a plant is referred to as a general category, the abbreviation "sp." is used instead of an individual species; "spp." indicates more than one unspecified species.

PART I

EVOLUTION OF A STYLE

INFLUENCES

My first taste of gardening came from mowing the lawn and pruning the ubiquitous shrubs around my family's suburban bungalow in Grand Rapids, Michigan, when I was a boy. The house had a small backyard, not more than twenty-five feet by thirty-five feet. I sharpened my gardening skills on the narrow flower beds that defined the perimeter of the yard. I remember experimenting with tea roses and a handful of perennials—bee balm, lily of the valley, phlox. My mother used to hang the weekly wash out to dry in the middle of our rectangular lawn. Following Dutch tradition, the wash was carefully arranged by size, from socks to sheets. The swaying laundry added a touch of color and movement to the garden.

When I was twelve I began a lawn-mowing business that soon expanded into the surrounding neighborhood. As my after-school business grew, I became fascinated by our neighbors' use of plants—especially their beautiful borders. Margaret Smith's lawn shrank to postage-stamp size as she enlarged her planting beds with larkspur, globe thistle, and iris. Marybell Pratt and Margaret Holmes had almost no lawn at all, even in front of their houses. In the 1940s, this was revolutionary. Instead, they had massive plantings of wake-robin, Turk's cap lily, and bluebells. My neighbors' enthusiasm for plants was contagious, and soon they began to share their plants with me when they divided them each spring. To my parents' chagrin, our prized backyard lawn gradually receded as I widened our planting beds and added

ABOVE: *Here I am at age two, already "gardening" at the foundation of our small suburban bungalow in Grand Rapids, Michigan.*
CORRINE SONNEVELDT PHOTOGRAPH

OPPOSITE: *My garden is lush and tropical in summer. Plants contribute to a feeling of limitless space by screening out the fences. The view from my kitchen through layers of* Magnolia virginiana *(sweet bay magnolia) in the foreground,* Miscanthus sinensis giganteus *(giant Chinese silver grass) in the center, and* Hamamelis mollis 'Brevipetala' *(Chinese witch hazel) in the back provides a welcome sense of mystery for such a small space.*

new plant varieties. Meanwhile, I welcomed the loss of the lawn, since I had developed a serious distaste for mowing.

My interest in horticulture increased when I discovered the pleasures of Michigan's glorious countryside. At age sixteen I began to draw and paint country meadows and wildflowers, as well as the sand dunes, grasses, and pines along the shores of Lake Michigan. Looking back, I realize now that painting expanded my vision of what a garden could be.

From the time I was a child my family would make an annual winter pilgrimage to Fort Myers, Florida, and it was in Florida that I discovered the beauty of formal, tropical gardens such as those at Cypress Gardens and the Schaddelee Estate, which has sadly long since been demolished. I have fond memories of running through palm allées and bougainvillea-covered arbors, through a series of outdoor rooms defined by hibiscus hedges and furnished with urns of cascading lantana.

At Wheaton College in Wheaton, Illinois, where I went to study liberal arts, I fell in love with architecture. Before my four years were up I had decided to become an architect, and I enrolled in architecture school at the University of Michigan in 1954. At Michigan I also studied town planning, which introduced me to landscape architecture, and I suddenly realized that the spaces between and around buildings interested me more than the buildings themselves. As soon as I finished my degree in architecture, I began a

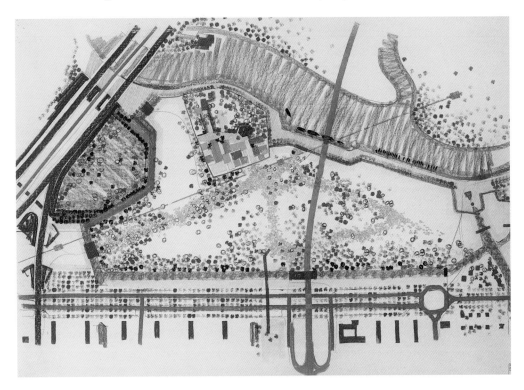

program in landscape architecture. And so I came around full circle: back to plants. But many years would pass before I took up a trowel and planted a garden again.

After Michigan, at my professor's recommendation, I studied landscape architecture at the University at Delft in the Netherlands with Jan Bijhouwer, one of the great landscape architects of our century. Professor Bijhouwer believed passionately in the natural evolution of a garden. He even planted gardens without paths, to allow people to move through them as they desired. Later, after "desire lines" appeared, he paved the paths and the gardens were complete. He taught me garden design on a grand scale. From him I gained a keen appreciation for natural, relaxed planting designs that relied on indigenous plants as well as North American wildflowers. Bijhouwer's love for the United States and its flora was contagious.

In February 1964, after three and a half years abroad, I was ready to return to the United States. Professor Bijhouwer told me as we parted that if I was ever near Baltimore, Maryland, I should look up a landscape architect he knew, Wolfgang Oehme. He had met Wolfgang on an International Federation of Landscape Architects tour in 1958. I dutifully took down his number and called him shortly after settling in Washington, D.C., in the spring of 1964. Our mutual love of Europe and fascination with plants and garden design fostered an instant friendship that strengthened over the next several years.

ABOVE: *Jeremiah D. O'Leary, Jr., city planner, at work with me on a downtown plan for Springfield, Massachusetts, c. 1968.*

OPPOSITE: *This is my first drawing for the Floriade Exhibition Grounds on the Amstel River, Amsterdam, Holland, c. 1961.*

During those years I worked as a landscape architect and urban designer in a city-planning consulting firm, Marcou, O'Leary and Associates, where I soon became a partner. At the same time, Wolfgang was sketching garden plans on backs of envelopes, hauling plants in the back of his car, digging, and single-handedly planting gardens. I envied his time outside and his rightful sense of accomplishment at seeing his designs come to life. I longed to join Wolfgang in planting gardens: new architectural commissions were rare at the time, and I too wanted to build my fantasies.

Wolfgang, who is German, had begun honing his gardening skills at the tender age of five in the small plot his family had rented from the city of Chemnitz, about a ten-minute walk from their flat. In it were a few fruit trees, gooseberry bushes, vegetables, annuals, and perennials. The walls cascaded with roses. Wolfgang's parents set a small section aside for him, where he planted his own garden of phlox, edelweiss, and ferns. He cultivated and fertilized his plants and worked his compost heap. His lifetime love of gardening had begun.

When Wolfgang was seventeen, he began apprenticing at the Max Illge Nursery in Bitterfeld, where he learned the basic skills of the trade, such as propagation and planting. But his love of perennials began with his first job, in the Bitterfeld Cemetery and Parks Department. It was during this time that he decided to become a landscape architect. The director, Hans Joachim Bauer, was his inspiration. Bauer is a landscape architect of great vision who knows his plants well, and together they visited and studied parks and botanic gardens. Bauer also introduced Wolfgang to the ideas of Karl Foerster. Foerster's great contribution was to make plants the most important element of the garden, especially perennials and grasses. He was highly sensitive to seasonal variations and promoted the garden as a place of learning. Both Wolfgang and I have been greatly inspired by Karl Foerster's work and writings.

Wolfgang enrolled in the landscape architecture program of the University of Berlin in 1952. Famous for its botanic gardens, Berlin is the capital of the horticulture field in Germany. Since World War II, the German government has held magnificent garden shows to reclaim war-devastated landscapes and cities. After graduating from the University of Berlin, Wolfgang became a member of the design team for the Hamburg National Garden Show, where he discovered the importance of public gardens in everyday life. It gave him a valuable glimpse of what plants can do for people.

When Wolfgang came to Baltimore in 1957, he found few interesting plants; perennials, and especially grasses, were scarce. He soon took to digging trees from the woods

around Baltimore, such as *Aralia spinosa*, and bringing seeds back in his pockets from his frequent trips to Europe. He gave the seeds to local nurserymen, who propagated them and allowed him to create the vast plant palette that makes our gardens unique.

In 1961, Wolfgang designed and planted a garden in Baltimore for Pauline Vollmer. Remembering the crude sketch and the unfamiliar list of plants he presented to her, she wonders now how she dared to build and plant such a garden. "It took great faith," she says. She boasts that the result is one of the most beautiful private gardens in America (see page 147).

(see page 147)

ABOVE: *Wolfgang and I return again and again to Planten un Bloemen, a 1,170-acre public park in Hamburg, Germany, for study and inspiration.* WOLFGANG OEHME PHOTOGRAPH

OPPOSITE: *Karl Foerster's garden in Potsdam, Germany, exemplifies his approach to planting design—layers of interesting plants used in a bold, painterly fashion.* PHOTOGRAPH C. 1930, COURTESY OF MARIANNE FOERSTER

On my first visit to Baltimore to meet Wolfgang and tour his gardens, he showed me the Vollmer garden. I'll never forget the moment I walked through the back gate. There was no lawn just a profusion of color and texture, the fluid movement of foliage and ornamental grasses. The planting was lush and dramatic, with colors ranging from dark green to soft blue-gray. In the summer light everything seemed to be in bloom, and the gentle afternoon breeze added to the enchantment. For the first time I saw how the movement of plants could integrate space and discovered the rich possibilities of great contrasts in scale, color, and foliage. Instantly, I was a believer.

Despite the stimulation of my work as an urban designer and landscape architect for a very successful city-planning consulting firm, I was ultimately unsatisfied with the results. For city planners, the political process is an end in itself, and during those years I rarely saw my designs constructed. My meeting with Wolfgang made me all the more aware of what I was missing.

In 1970, I bought an old two-story Victorian row house in Georgetown, a historic neighborhood in Washington, D.C., just twelve blocks from the White House. I live there still. The lot is just seventeen feet wide and one hundred and forty feet deep. By 1971, I was ready to design and build a garden to replace the tiny lawn and twenty rosebushes that I had inherited. I called Wolfgang and suggested we do it together. The back garden is fifty-five feet deep, and my preliminary drawing included a small terrace, seven feet deep, stretching across the back of the house off the kitchen. Since the ground plane slopes upward I added a low retaining wall to the back of the terrace and five steps leading up to a gently curving path of concrete stepping stones. Wolfgang sketched the layout for the plants. We discussed the drawings over lunch, made minor adjustments, and I was ready to begin. I had some stonemason friends build the "hardscape," or infrastructure. When that was finished, Wolfgang located all the plants at his neighborhood nursery and brought them to my house in the back of his Volkswagen station wagon. We planted the garden together on a Saturday afternoon. The entire garden was completed in less than one week. So began a collaboration that continues to this day.

Almost immediately, my garden became a showplace. No one had ever seen anything quite like it. From the kitchen the view of the various layers is stunning and mysterious. In the foreground is a *Magnolia virginiana* (sweet bay magnolia); one-third and two-thirds of the way back stand clumps of *Miscanthus sinensis giganteus,* and against the back fence, a *Hamamelis mollis* 'Brevipetala' (Chinese witch hazel). The lawn and roses gave way to a carpet of shrubs and perennials. The high canopy of the *Ailanthus altissima* (tree of heaven) gives the space a tropical quality, while the borrowed scenery of the neighbors' gardens extends the view far beyond the fence.

Luckily, the garden's natural upward tilt fools the eye with a false perspective, like a raked stage. Even in a very small space Wolfgang and I had proved that not everything has to be revealed at once: there could still be surprises. As I looked out from my kitchen, I thought that there had to be a demand for gardens like this. I was right (see page 2).

Working with Wolfgang on my garden convinced me that this was what I wanted to do for a living. In 1975, we formally announced our partnership and I resigned from the firm, and on the strength of my garden alone we had five clients within the first year.

Wolfgang and I complement each other in training and expertise, covering the spectrum from architecture to horticulture. We learned fast, sometimes through mistakes, but we were able to experiment and adjust because we installed the gardens ourselves. Our drawings were sketchy and we did a great deal of creative work in the field, just as most gardeners do. No one wanted to pay for a set of plans at the time, so we made our living by planting gardens, not by designing them.

But even on our first commissions, we experimented with some of the influences we had both gathered from abroad. Mien Ruys, a Dutch landscape architect who began her practice more than seventy years ago, influenced our feeling for residential scale. Rejecting formal borders with beds of annuals, Ruys's planting designs feature large, free, informal drifts of color. In the Netherlands, she and Professor Bijhouwer pioneered a movement toward landscapes that are strong in concept, carefully detailed, and overlaid with a soft, natural palette of plants. I was also influenced by the strong "picturesque" gardens of Lancelot (Capability) Brown (1715–1783), which I had a chance to visit while studying in Europe. They were moody, and designed on a grand scale: plants were moved about and landscapes were entirely reconstructed to improve on nature and to create a series of perfect "pictures." His stunning, bold vision revolutionized spatial design.

Roberto Burle Marx (1909–1993), the brilliant Brazilian landscape architect and artist, told me in 1987, when I visited him in Rio de Janeiro, that he too had been greatly inspired as a young man by Capability Brown's landscapes, and especially by Blenheim Park in Oxfordshire. Roberto and I also shared an appreciation for the herbaceous borders of Gertrude Jekyll (1843–1932), who was trained as a painter and considered her designs

Wolfgang and I pose at the back of my station wagon, which is stocked with shrubs and perennials ready to be planted in the Blair garden in Washington, D.C.
ARLINKA BLAIR
PHOTOGRAPH, c. 1975

Top: In her garden in the Netherlands, Mien Ruys creates depth by layering plants of contrasting foliage, size, and color.

Above: Roberto Burle Marx arranged plants in bold paisley patterns for this private garden in Petropolis, Brazil.

Opposite: At the Ministry of Justice in Brasilia, Brazil, Roberto Burle Marx used plants with dramatically contrasting leaf size and color.

"paintings on the ground plane." Roberto was also a painter. He laid his plants in colorful abstract patterns. Roberto and I also shared a deep respect for the work of Karl Foerster.

Burle Marx's tropical gardens have influenced our work for many years. During my 1987 visit, he generously took me to see many of his gardens in and around Rio de Janeiro. It was clear to me then that he was linking the dramatic "borrowed scenery" of Rio to his gardens with abstract forms and native plants. The Monteiro Garden, in Petropolis, Brazil, is a perfect example of his method, and I am convinced that we shared a common vision.

My appreciation for grasses by now a trademark of an Oehme, van Sweden garden can be traced back to my studies in the Netherlands and was nurtured by a fruitful visit to Japan in 1983, where I went to see *Miscanthus sinensis* and other Japanese grasses growing in their native habitat. The Japanese have valued grasses for over a thousand years and have used their grasses for roofing, tatami mats, baskets, and many other purposes. They celebrate the all-season beauty of grasses in many art forms: paintings, textiles, lacquered surfaces, and screens.

For the Japanese, time's seasonal effect on the garden is paramount. Each plant must be contemplated in its evolution throughout the season, and its placement in space decided accordingly. While I enjoy Japanese gardens on a purely physical level, the subtle placement of every element—plant, stone, ornament—is what greatly enhances my enjoyment.

In the United States, my principal influences have been the "Prairie School" of Frank Lloyd Wright (1867–1959), the natural and ecologically friendly landscape designs of Jens Jensen (1890–1950), and, of course, the work of the great Frederick Law Olmsted (1822–1903).

Jens Jensen garden, Glencoe, Illinois.

A number of contemporary American designers share our interest in a natural, relaxed, bold landscape designed with grasses and a rich palette of plants. Darrel Morrison, professor of landscape architecture at the University of Georgia and an early proponent of using native grasses in designed landscapes, has been a great inspiration to me since the 1970s. Over the years, he has generously shared his vast knowledge of prairie and meadow restoration with Wolfgang and me, and he has been instrumental in reviving our country's aesthetic and ecological interest in native grasses. Another home-grown naturalist is A. E. Bye, whose designs reinforce the natural character of their setting with the utmost simplicity. In one of his earliest gardens, at Long Beach, on the coast of New Jersey, he shaped the dunes and seeded them with *Ammophila breviligulata* (beach grass). Then he added dark, undulating masses of *Pinus thunbergiana* (Japanese black pine) and *Myrica pensylvanica* (northern bayberry). The result is sculptural and dramatic.

Another crucial influence came from outside the world of landscape architecture. I have always loved the landscapes and interiors of the early Dutch masters, with their

*ABOVE: Shibata Zeshin (1807–1891), gilt screen
Autumn Grasses. The Metropolitan Museum of Art,
The Harry G. C. Packard Collection of Asian Art,
Gift of Harry G. C. Packard, and Purchase, Fletcher,
Rogers, Harris Brisbane Dick and Louis V. Bell
Funds, Joseph Pulitzer Bequest and The Annenberg
Fund, Inc. Gift, 1975. (1975.268.137). Photo-
graph © 1990 by The Metropolitan Museum of Art.*

*RIGHT: Miscanthus sinensis in its native habitat —
a mountainside on the island of Honshu, Japan.*

rich lessons in light, texture, color, and proportion, and the bold and vibrant works of contemporary painters. I look to the hard-edged paintings of David Hockney and Edward Hopper for images of the American landscape—from clipped hedges and sheared lawns in California to the lawn "gone to seed" in New England. But I draw inspiration from nonfigurative painters as well: the dynamism of works by Helen Frankenthaler, Hans Hofmann, and Frank Stella encouraged me to plant on a big scale and inspired my landscape design. In Frankenthaler's paintings large masses of color sweep across the canvas, blurring the edges where they meet. In Hans Hofmann's paintings, rectangular forms float in swirling pools of color before colliding in a sharp contrast of hard edges. Jazzy use of collage and paint distinguish the canvases of Frank Stella.

All my life I have enjoyed and studied the arts—architecture, music, sculpture, painting, dance. I have tried to integrate lessons from each of these in my designs. Always, they refresh and feed my creative juices. The New American Garden style is inspired by my interests in the arts, travel, and study of other gardening traditions, as well as by many years of practice with Wolfgang.

ABOVE: *Having obviously stopped mowing their lawn, this couple observes a soft grassy meadow that stretches far back into the woods.(Edward Hopper,* Cape Cod Evening, *1939. John Hay Whitney Collection, National Gallery of Art, Washington.)*

OPPOSITE TOP: *Darrel Morrison's design for this prairie at the University of Wisconsin Arboretum in Madison, Wisconsin, features native grasses and perennials.*
DARREL MORRISON PHOTOGRAPH, C. 1975

OPPOSITE BOTTOM: *A. E. Bye shaped these dunes on the Atlantic Ocean, seeded them with dune grass, and planted dark accents to reinforce the natural character of the site.*
A. E. BYE PHOTOGRAPH

David Hockney, A Neat Lawn, 1967. Acrylic.
96" × 96" © David Hockney

THE NEW
AMERICAN GARDEN

Americans crave frontiers. We like wide-open spaces, broad horizons, and new challenges. As a nation, we are restless wanderers, always searching for what's over the next rise. We put down roots only to pull them up again when the spirit moves us.

Given our love of change, it's surprising that the American garden scene consists mostly of urban and suburban yards marching across the countryside in uniform ranks: hedges pruned carefully into unnatural boxes and balls; "foundation" shrubs piled high against houses like green concrete; broad, empty lawns awaiting weekly crew cuts and frequent doses of weed killer and water; and prissy flower beds jammed to their borders with garish and predictable annuals. Do gardens have to be so tame, so harnessed, so uptight?

Happily for Wolfgang and me, this long dry spell in contemporary gardening history is giving way to a new movement toward more relaxed, less formulaic, and more natural landscapes, and toward a new aesthetic that has come to be known as the New American Garden style.* Wolfgang and I see the new garden style that we helped pioneer as an American melting pot of international plants and ideas.† When applied on a grand scale to public and private spaces it results in gardens that are natural, free-spirited, and often wild. Its point of reference is the American meadow—a place of freedom and ease where wildlife, plant life, and human life coexist in harmony. After twenty years of implementing our vision, we have come to see it as a revolution in gardening.

---

* Our gardens have been given many labels, including the "Laissez-faire Garden," the "New Romantic Garden," the "Four Seasons Garden," "Gardens of Delight," "Bold Romantic Gardens," and "New World Gardens," but the "New American Garden" is the label that has caught on to describe this new style of landscaping.

† We subtitled our first book *New World Landscapes* to reflect our international palette of plants. As I wrote in a letter to the editor of the *Washington Post* (June 2, 1988), "Can anyone take seriously a suggestion that we return to the plant palette existing before Columbus and tell American garden designers past and present that combinations of imports and natives as seen in their gardens for hundreds of years are 'contrived'?"

What's new about our New American Garden is what's new about America itself: it is vigorous and audacious, and it vividly blends the natural and the cultivated. It is relaxed and rich, and it celebrates seasonal change.

In the New American Garden we blur edges and allow plants to grow together. We encourage the intermixing of species over time, such as *Rudbeckia fulgida* 'Goldsturm' seeding among the *Pennisetum alopecuroides*. Our gardens are low-maintenance (notice I say *low*—not *no*): we do not overmaintain and we discourage the unnatural-looking "fine-toothed comb" approach. We do not carve shrubs and trees into artificial shapes but allow them to develop naturally, pruning them only to enhance their sculptural beauty. Our gardens require a minimum of water after they are established, and we use herbicides and pesticides only as a last resort.

Most important, our gardens retain their drama through each change of season. During spring and summer plants are al-

Top: When Wolfgang and I started the redesign of Freedom Plaza in Washington, D.C, in 1981, it had twenty-one alcoves of yews carved into rigid and boring hedges that resembled blocks of "green concrete."

Middle: A happy day came in 1984 when we were permitted to remove the yews. I consider this day the beginning of the New American Garden revolution in America.

Bottom: Detail of an alcove replanted with a collection of perennials and shrubs and silhouetted against newly exposed granite in two shades of mauve. Robert Venturi, architect, asked that his aluminum urns, one of which is seen here, be planted to look like Edwardian women's hats.

RICHARD FELBER

lowed to flourish naturally without pruning, staking, deadheading, or dividing. By fall they are lush with autumnal colors and the abundant forms of seed heads, stalks, and leaves. This develops into a wonderful winter garden that lasts until spring announces a new cycle of growth.

Many Americans view the dried winter garden as a dead garden. Evergreens are considered alive in winter and are often used in excess to compensate for lack of green. The result is what Wolfgang and I call the "plastic evergreen look." The New American Garden is beautiful in all seasons, including the winter, when it is virtually a dried bouquet. To our surprise, many people consider our gardens more beautiful in winter—when the contrast between evergreen and deciduous plants is especially appealing—than in any other season.

Our gardens are dynamic; they move in the breeze and sparkle like stained glass in the sunlight. Their magical fluidity is achieved through the interrelationship of plants, combined in both horizontal and vertical planes. The New American Garden is best appreciated while standing in the midst of it, surrounded by plants on all sides. We have neither "foundation plants" nor "perennial borders" because we treat the entire ground plane as an integrated whole. No more piling of plants against the foundation of the house, no more useless lawns that carpet the empty space out to the curb. Instead, plants should radiate from the house in all directions like a great tapestry or collage, and the lawn should be confined to as small an area as possible and used only for specific activities, such as sunbathing, croquet, or children's play (my rule of thumb: limit lawn size so that you can cut it comfortably with an old-fashioned push mower).

The New American Garden reflects the beauties of the American countryside, especially its meadows and prairies. It follows in the tradition of environmentally friendly gardens that minimize the use of water and chemicals while nurturing and encouraging wildlife. But most important, it should stimulate your senses and fill your imagination—just as it reminds me from time to time of the pleasure of a fragrant breeze while hiking over lakeside dunes, across farm pastures, and through meadows of wildflowers and grasses on warm summer days.

RICHARD FELBER

PART II
PLANTING OUR GARDENS

ELEMENTS OF DESIGN

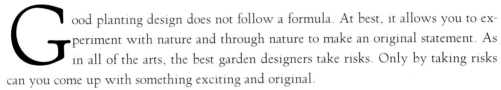

ood planting design does not follow a formula. At best, it allows you to experiment with nature and through nature to make an original statement. As in all of the arts, the best garden designers take risks. Only by taking risks can you come up with something exciting and original.

We are fortunate to have had many clients willing to go out on a limb. Many of our clients are involved in the arts and are therefore open to experimental designs and concepts. Many share our weariness with the predictable lawn and mixed border.

Regardless of whether the garden is public or private, Wolfgang and I always begin our planting schemes by learning about our clients' practical requirements and favorite plants. Then we try to see how their tastes can be integrated into our vision. We often draw from previous commissions, but we see each garden as an opportunity to expand our repertoire.

A garden is not like a new automobile that depreciates once you drive it out of the showroom: a newly planted garden can only appreciate in beauty. Changes occur daily from the time it is planted, and with proper care it improves dramatically every day. Wolfgang and I have often been surprised by what has happened to our planting schemes over time. In many ways, once planted, the garden's progress is out of our hands.

The amount of money you decide to spend on your garden will determine how patient you will have to be. Your budget dictates how long you will have to wait for your garden to reach maturity by determining, for example, the size of trees and shrubs, the maturity of perennials, and how far apart they will be planted. Instant gratification comes at a cost.

Wolfgang and I apply a few rules of thumb in beginning to draw a planting scheme. First we consider the site's natural framework. Following the Japanese tradition, we search for surrounding views to feature as "borrowed scenery": distant hills, a body of water, or even major trees on a neighbor's property. Next we take note of interesting features in the natural topography, such as the site's orientation to sunlight, breezes, and the quality of light at various times of day. Then we test the soil and carefully study the garden's climatic zone.

We begin our planting schemes by drawing in major design features, such as trees, shrubs, and large ornamental grasses. Large trees give the garden an overhead canopy.

Top: The combination of dried Liatris spicata *seed heads and waning* Hibiscus moscheutos *(rose mallow) foretell the coming of autumn.*
ROGER FOLEY PHOTOGRAPH

ABOVE: We planted this colorful meadow on Maryland's Eastern Shore with a combination of plants such as Daucus carota *(Queen Anne's lace),* Liatris spicata, Rudbeckia fulgida, *and* Echinacea purpurea.
JEFFREY A. CHARLESWORTH PHOTOGRAPH

OPPOSITE: In autumn the evergreen Yucca filamentosa *emerges in sharp contrast to the russet gray and brown tones of perennials drying and going to seed.*
ROGER FOLEY PHOTOGRAPH

Smaller trees, shrubs, and grasses, placed singly and in groups, give structure to the garden, provide focal points, and frame views. Smaller plants soften walls, subdivide spaces, create transitions, and establish boundaries. We depend on the sculptural qualities of the plants to create patterns of tension, balance, and rhythm that pull the visitor visually and physically through the garden.

Next we fill in the ground plane with herbaceous perennials. These are the plants that create our lush and undulating "ground cover." Plant varieties in this "lower tier" range from species that hug the ground, such as *Mazus reptans* (blue mazus) or *Molinia litorialis* 'Transparent', which blooms seven feet in the air. Taller specimens within these broad masses subdivide the planting into different layers that then move in all directions. While the overall size of these plant masses may change as they develop, the size of specific perennials and their relative proportion to each other will not change. We rarely include annuals in the planting areas, recommending instead that they be planted in containers to give color throughout the summer season.

A garden's sense of drama can be accentuated by using plants with contrasting leaf size. For example, we may combine the platelike green leaves of *Petasites japonicus* (Japanese butterbur) with the fine-textured, blue-gray mounds of *Festuca glauca* (blue fescue). Because we like people to touch the plants in their gardens we choose those with interesting leaf texture, such as the velvety *Stachys byzantina* (lamb's ears) and the fuzzy efflorescence of *Panicum virgatum*. Everyone loves color, so we use plants that are beautiful in flower. However, the full color range of leaves and dried seed heads from early spring through winter is just as important to us. Examples include the lettuce-green foliage of *Mazus reptans* in summer and the fiery crimson of *Miscanthus sinensis purpurascens* during autumn.

To connect the garden with its surroundings we place plants in broad, sweeping masses. At the same time, we design our gardens to be enjoyed at close range. These are spaces to be lived in, not just looked at, so we design comfortable places within the garden from which it can be enjoyed. From the house, a terrace, or a bench, our gardens radiate out with increasing simplicity until the distant view dissolves into a vast meadow (note the Feldman Garden on Martha's Vineyard, p. 42). This technique pulls the garden together and integrates it with its surroundings. It works in varying degrees at every scale, even in my own small plot in Washington, D.C. (p. 2).

We put all of these concepts on paper to present our "big idea" to the client, measure by square foot the areas of plantings, and prepare an accurate cost estimate. Our dynamic and sculptural planting schemes owe a great deal to the fact that we place the plants on the ground ourselves. Wolfgang and I use our drawings as a guide, never as ends in themselves. When the garden is planted we update the drawings to show the site as it is actually planted. This final, "as-built" plan is an important record for future reference.

In a finished garden, trees, grasses, and shrubs should present themselves gradually, unfold slowly, and never be visible all at once. When we enter a garden we want to feel as though we are uncovering a mystery whose layers we peel off one by one. Foliage should obscure an intriguing hiding place as well as provide shade.

Wolfgang and I design on a bold scale. Plant sizes, fruits, flowers, and leaves should never be skimpy, even in a small garden: designing small only intensifies the tightness of the garden space. Massed plantings in larger gardens should be grand in proportion, dramatic in scale, and laid out in huge swaths and with varying heights of color and texture.

Instead of specifying just ten or twenty or fifty plants for a given space, we think in terms of hundreds or even thousands. Nonetheless, often the larger the garden, the fewer the plant species we will use. In such cases, we prefer bold and simple designs.

We choose plants that change dramatically in color and form with each season. Spring brings a splash of color that I like to think of as "fireworks." Anyone can do spring. Toss a few bulbs over the planted area among the perennials in autumn, plant them where they fall, and you will have a beautiful spring garden. The bulbs will push up after the dried winter garden has been cut down and bloom among the emerging summer garden. As summer unfolds, the garden fills up. Mulch slowly disappears beneath the new bursts of growth. Grasses thicken, and the flowers emerge in profusion. Many plants, such as *Polygonum aubertii* and *Sedum* x 'Autumn Joy', draw bees, while *Ligularia dentata* 'Desdemona' and *Buddleia davidii* (butterfly bush) attract butterflies. Any garden in which *Ligularia dentata* 'Desdemona' is in bloom will be covered with monarch butterflies. The fragrance of flowers such as *Lonicera periclymenum* (woodbine honeysuckle) is intoxicating. In my own garden, the scent of *Magnolia virginiana* (sweet bay magnolia) blossoms perfumes the terrace in the cool of the evening, while the cicadas sing from my *Ailanthus altissima* (tree of heaven).

In autumn, the garden's colors ripen, and seed heads form almost imperceptibly as leaves begin to dry (notice I say *dry,* not *die*). Evergreen plants begin to emerge in contrast to the pale leaves of grasses going golden and red. Seed heads turn chocolate brown and mauve. We have found that combining one-third evergreen plants with two-thirds deciduous perennials gives just the right amount of green in autumn and winter.

Most herbaceous plants remain beautiful and interesting throughout the winter months. Stalks of wheat-colored dried grasses stand like sentinels, rustling in the breeze, while dried seed heads add sculptural interest and feed the birds. Even in winter the stark beauty of our gardens makes them remarkably inviting.

ROGER FOLEY

Time is the gardener's friend and foe, always working its relentless changes. Gardening teaches us patience—who can forget waiting for their first grapefruit seed to sprout in a mud-filled Dixie cup? But gardens also can teach us to live more in the moment—to listen, to watch, to touch, and to dream as the garden works its peaceful magic.

Portfolio of Gardens

The Blumer-Martin Garden

Dancing Point

The Diamond Garden

The Feldman Garden

Francis Scott Key Park

The Gratz Garden

The Corbin and Jean Gwaltney Garden

The Hamowy Garden

The Helms Garden

The Wendell and Dorothy Hester Garden

International Chancery Center

The Jacobs Garden

The Jerald J. Littlefield Garden

The Marsh Estate Garden

The Mr. and Mrs. Ulrich Meyer Garden

New American and Friendship Gardens

The Oehme Garden

The Mr. and Mrs. Nelson Offutt Garden

Paradise Manor Apartments

The Richard and Carole Rifkind Garden

Nelson A. Rockefeller Park

The Carole and Alex Rosenberg Terrace

The Simon and Rosita Trinca Garden

The Susan and John Ulfelder Garden

Virginia Avenue Gardens of the Federal Reserve System

The Leo and Pauline Vollmer Garden

Washington National Airport South Parking Garage

W orking with clients to restore neglected resources is a rewarding challenge, and discovering unexpected beauty is always a thrill. The Blumer-Martin project was especially satisfying. We started with unmistakable potential: a charming hundred-year-old English cottage on a large and steeply sloping site in New England.

Our first impression of the house and site did not match the story-book image that it deserved. Untended vines and other "foundation" planting diminished

The
Blumer-Martin
Garden
~❧~

the charm of the historic architecture. A long driveway disrupted usable spaces and views as it wound around the house to a rear garage. Overgrown plants at the back of the site obscured potential views of the adjacent tidal marsh. There were no outdoor living opportunities, and the approach to the house was undistinguished except for an interesting, but unimproved, garden space defined by a low stone wall.

A river of lawn sweeps down a gentle slope to the wetlands of Long Island Sound between massive plantings of Petasites japonicus (Japanese butterbur) and Calamagrostis acutiflora stricta.
RICHARD FELBER PHOTOGRAPH

With so many resources at hand it was fun to start setting them in order. We relocated the driveway to the opposite side of the house, where it is more direct and less visible. We opened views at the back of the site to the tidal marsh. We created a shade garden in front to block views of the road. We designed outdoor living terraces and connected them with broad stone steps that

The front of the house as seen from the driveway.

move easily from level to level. Finally, we tied the whole composition together with swirls of lawn that encircle the house and create an exaggerated feeling of spaciousness.

After resolving the broader site issues we moved on to the walled space outside the front door and created the garden's exclamation point. We had targeted this space at the beginning as a centerpiece for the entire garden—a jewel in the center of the property where visitors are introduced not only to the carefully restored and expanded cottage but to the rest of the garden as well. First, we drew attention to the entrance by adding a sweeping walkway that connects it to the front driveway. Where the walk enters the existing walled space, we added stone piers with caps on either side. Thus enclosed, the space takes on the feeling of an outdoor room. We furthered the illusion by adding a beautiful teak bench. Of course, we left plenty of perimeter space for lush planting.

RICHARD FELBER

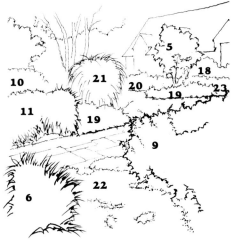

In keeping with the architectural style, we envisioned the small entrance garden as an English cottage garden with an American low-maintenance twist. The plant list includes *Buddleia davidii* 'Nanho Purple' (butterfly bush), *Echinops ritro* 'Taplow Blue' (globe thistle), *Lavandula angustifolia* 'Hidcote' (lavender), *Monarda didyma* 'Purpurkrone' (purple bee balm), and *Stachys byzantina* 'Helene von Stein' (lamb's ears).

Terry Blumer and Judy Martin wanted a unique garden and were eager participants with us in its design. "We thought it was a great process," Judy says. As the garden matures they continue to share their enthusiasm with Wolfgang and me. Judy joins patient gardeners everywhere when she says, "I'm prepared to watch things grow."

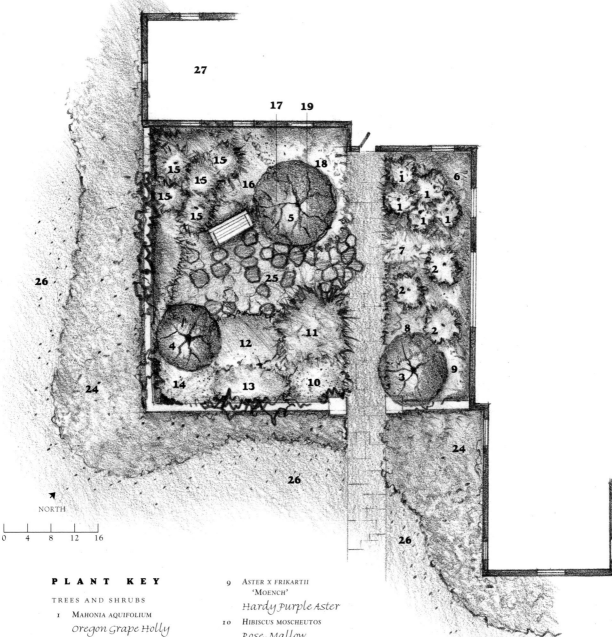

NORTH

0 4 8 12 16

PLANT KEY

TREES AND SHRUBS

1 MAHONIA AQUIFOLIUM
   Oregon Grape Holly

2 BUDDLEIA DAVIDII
   Butterfly Bush

3 STEWARTIA PSEUDOCAMELLIA
   Japanese Stewartia

4 CHIONANTHUS RETUSUS
   Chinese Fringetree

5 MAGNOLIA VIRGINIANA
   Sweetbay Magnolia

PERENNIALS AND
   ORNAMENTAL GRASSES

6 LIRIOPE MUSCARI 'BIG BLUE'
   Big Blue Lilyturf

7 HEMEROCALLIS SP.
   Daylily

8 LAVANDULA ANGUSTIFOLIA 'HIDCOTE'
   Lavender

9 ASTER X FRIKARTII
   'MOENCH'
   Hardy Purple Aster

10 HIBISCUS MOSCHEUTOS
   Rose Mallow

11 PENNISETUM ALOPECUROIDES
   'HAMELN'
   Dwarf Fountain Grass

12 MONARDA DIDYMA 'PURPURKRONE'
   Purple Beebalm

13 EUPHORBIA AMYGDALOIDES 'ROBBIAE'
   Wood Spurge

14 ASTILBE JAPONICA
   False Spiraea

15 FARGESIA NITIDA
   Blue Clump Bamboo

16 HELLEBORUS ORIENTALIS
   Lenten Rose

17 NEPETA X FAASSENII
   Catnip

18 ECHINOPS RITRO 'TAPLOW BLUE'
   Globe Thistle

19 STACHYS BYZANTINA 'HELENE VON
   STEIN'
   Lamb's Ear

20 PEROVSKIA ATRIPLICIFOLIA
   Russian Sage

21 MISCANTHUS SINENSIS
   Silver Grass

22 MAZUS REPTANS
   Blue Mazus

23 SEDUM X 'AUTUMN JOY'
   Stonecrop

MISCELLANEOUS

24 PERENNIAL MASSING

25 STONE TERRACE

26 LAWN

27 RESIDENCE

T he lapping waters of the James River define three sides of Dancing Point, this aptly named peninsula in Virginia's Tidewater country. The contemporary house features expansive glass walls that expose visitors to striking views of the river and distant forests.

We began our design by studying the architecture of the house, its immediate surroundings, and the "borrowed" scenery. We were struck by the site's exposure to competing visual attractions: lake-like expanses of water, intermittent movement of river traffic, and reflections of dramatic skies. We concluded that

DANCING POINT

these competing views should not confront the visitor all at once but should be disclosed in a carefully controlled sequence. Our planting scheme achieves this by setting up visual tensions between selected distant views and foreground features. An arbor at the outer edge of the dining room lawn is a good example; cascading with honeysuckle and clematis, it frames distant views and provides alluring foreground interest. The owner has

The contrasting bold texture and bright yellow color of Helianthus angustifolius (swamp sunflower) break the edge between the land and the mirrored blue surface of the James River.

told us that the planted arbor provides "a lovely place to sit, like a lookout, with flowers overhead."

The owner asked for white, lavender, and watermelon-pink flowers. We obliged by planting masses of *Eupatorium purpureum* (joe-pye weed), *Hibiscus moscheutos* (rose mallow), *Anemone japonica* (Japanese anemone), *Astilbe* sp. (false spirea), *Iris sibirica* (Siberian iris), *Paeonia* sp. (peony), and *Lagerstroemia indica* (crape myrtle). Great sweeps of pastel colors now flow from the house to the river's azure-blue water.

Late in his career, the great California landscape architect Thomas Church created the master plan for this property. We were honored to fulfill his vision.

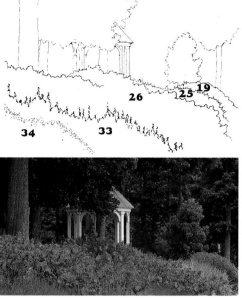

Roger Foley

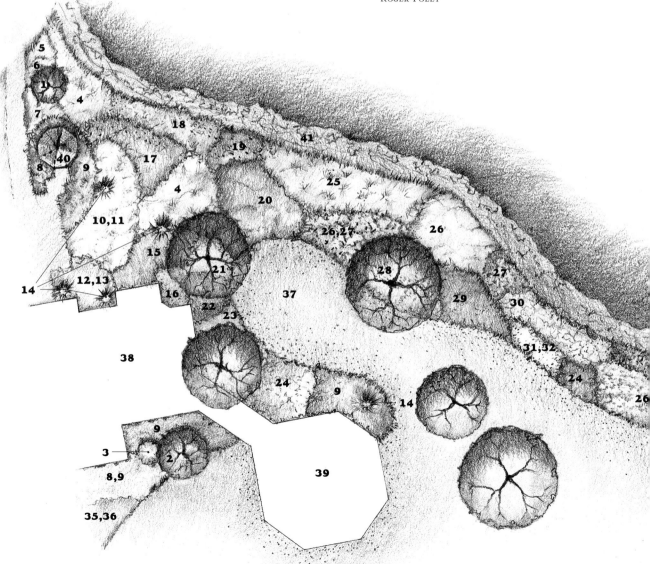

PLANT KEY

TREES AND SHRUBS

1 MAGNOLIA VIRGINIANA
  Sweet Bay Magnolia

2 QUERCUS VIRGINIANA
  Live Oak

3 HAMAMELIS X INTERMEDIA 'ARNOLD PROMISE'
  Witch Hazel

PERENNIALS AND ORNAMENTAL GRASSES

4 HEMEROCALLIS SPP.
  Daylily

5 ACANTHUS HUNGARICUS
  Bear's-Breech

6 SEDUM X 'AUTUMN JOY'
  Stonecrop

7 CHRYSANTHEMUM PACIFICUM
  Gold and Silver Chrysanthemum

8 AGAPANTHUS UMBELLATUS 'BLUE TRIUMPHATOR'
  Lily of the Nile

9 LIRIOPE MUSCARI 'BIG BLUE'
  Lily-Turf

10 DRYOPTERIS ERYTHROSORA
  Autumn Fern

11 ASARUM SUPERBUM
  Wild Ginger

12 HERBS

13 HOSTA X 'HONEYBELLS'
  Plantain Lily

14 FARGESIA NITIDA
  Blue Clump Bamboo

15 ANEMONE JAPONICA 'HONORINE JOBERT'
  White Japanese Anemone

16 EPIMEDIUM SPP.
  Barrenwort

17 PENNISETUM ALOPECUROIDES 'MOUDRY'
  Fountain Grass

18 LYSIMACHIA CLETHROIDES
  Gooseneck Loosestrife

19 EUPATORIUM PURPUREUM
  Joe-Pye Weed

20 VERONICA LONGIFOLIA 'SUNNY BORDER BLUE'
  Blue Speedwell

21 BERGENIA CRASSIFOLIA 'RED STAR'
  Leather Bergenia

22 CHELONE LYONII
  Turtle-Head

23 ASTER X FRIKARTII 'MÖNCH'
  Hardy Purple Aster

24 PHYSOSTEGIA VIRGINIANA 'VIVID'
  False Dragonhead

25 CALAMAGROSTIS ACUTIFLORA STRICTA
  Feather Reed Grass

26 HIBISCUS MOSCHEUTOS
  Rose Mallow

27 BOLTONIA ASTEROIDES 'SNOWBANK'
  White Boltonia

28 HELIANTHUS ANGUSTIFOLIUS
  Swamp Sunflower

29 SPODIOPOGON SIBIRICUS
  Silver Spike Grass

30 PEROVSKIA ATRIPLICIFOLIA
  Russian Sage

31 COREOPSIS VERTICILLATA
  Yellow Tickseed

32 LIATRIS SPICATA
  Gayfeather

33 LYTHRUM SALICARIA 'MORDEN'S PINK'
  Loosestrife

34 PANICUM VIRGATUM
  Switch Grass

35 GERANIUM X 'BIOKOVO'
  Biokovo Geranium

36 ANEMONE JAPONICA 'PAMINA'
  Rose Pink Japanese Anemone

MISCELLANEOUS

37 LAWN

38 RESIDENCE

39 LIVING ROOM PAVILLION

40 GAZEBO

41 RIPRAP (STONE BEACH PROTECTION)

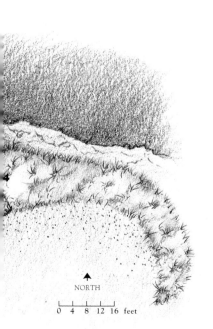

NORTH

0 4 8 12 16 feet

ROGER FOLEY

Early in our practice, Wolfgang and I agreed on a fundamental rule: never try to compete with a site's natural beauty. Instead, adopt its given attributes and let the beauty of the site shine through. Our design for the Diamonds' thirty-six-acre exurban property in Westchester County, New York, followed this principle.

The site's natural features include an isolated bluff surrounded by rugged topography, forty-foot rock outcroppings, and towering stands of native trees. The Diamonds' quietly

THE DIAMOND GARDEN

elegant shingle house commands spectacular views of the countryside from its setting near the crest of the bluff.

All our improvements are sympathetic to the site. An entrance drive winds through the forest and around a hilltop "meadow" before arriving at the house. The "meadow" is a natural disguise for a required septic field. Plantings on the septic field's shallow cover include *Monarda didyma* 'Purpurkrone' (purple bee balm), *Cimicifuga racemosa, Aconitum carmichaelii* (monkshood), *Clethra alnifolia* 'Hummingbird' (summersweet clethra), and *Helianthus angustifolius* (swamp sunflower).

The entrance drive terminates at a forecourt, where a rustic boulder retaining wall and broad granite steps define an elevated en-

RICHARD FELBER

RICHARD FELBER

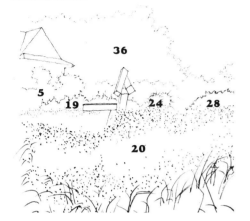

trance garden. The entrance garden is the first in a progression of connected garden spaces around the house. Each merges imperceptibly with its natural surroundings. A meandering system of rustic stone paths connects the garden to more than thirty acres of woodlands.

We chose a rich palette of plants that would adapt to the garden's varying conditions of shade and sun, and to its meadow, forest, pools, and containers. The plants we selected for resistance to deer—beautiful but voracious visitors—include *Geranium macrorrhizum, Ligularia dentata* 'Desdemona', *Senecio aureus,* and many grasses and ferns. The Diamonds also installed a nine-foot chain-link fence at the perimeter of the garden to further discourage deer. Surprisingly, but effectively, there is no lawn in this large garden.

PLANT KEY

TREES AND SHRUBS

1 RHODODENDRON MUCRONULATUM
  Korean Rhododendron
2 AMELANCHIER CANADENSIS 'ROBINHILL PINK'
  Pink Shadblow Serviceberry
3 THUGA OCCIDENTALIS 'TECHNY'
  American Arborvitae
4 CLETHRA ALNIFOLIA 'HUMMINGBIRD'
  Summersweet
5 SYRINGA RETICULATA
  Japanese Tree Lilac

PERENNIALS AND ORNAMENTAL GRASSES

6 SENECIO AUREUS
  Golden Groundsel
7 EPIMEDIUM RUBRUM
  Barrenwort
8 LYSIMACHIA CLETHROIDES
  Gooseneck Loosestrife
9 GERANIUM PLATYPETALUM
  Wild Cranesbill
10 HELLEBORUS ORIENTALIS
  Lenten Rose

11 POLYSTICHUM ACROSTICHOIDES
  Christmas Fern
12 TRACHYSTEMON ORIENTALE
  Eastern Borage
13 ASTILBE JAPONICA 'DEUTSCHLAND'
  White False Spiraea
14 FARGESIA NITIDA
  Blue Clump Bamboo
15 BRUNNERA MACROPHYLLA
  Siberian Bugloss
16 LIGULARIA DENTATA 'DESDEMONA'
  Goldenray
17 MOLINIA LITORIALIS 'TRANSPARENT'
  Purple Moor Grass
18 CIMICIFUGA RACEMOSA
  Black Snakeroot
19 POLYGONUM POLYMORPHUM
  Fleece Flower
20 PANICUM VIRGATUM 'HAENSE HERMS'
  Red Switch Grass
21 CIMICIFUGA AMERICANA
  Bugbane
22 EUPATORIUM FISTULOSUM 'GATEWAY'
  Joe-Pye Weed
23 PENNISETUM ALOPECUROIDES
  Fountain Grass

24 MISCANTHUS SINENSIS GIGANTEUS
  Giant Chinese Silver Grass
25 CAMPANULA PERSICIFOLIA
  Peach-leaf Bellflower
26 ASTER DIVARICATUS
  White Wood Aster
27 MONARDA DIDYMA 'PURPURKRONE'
  Purple Bee Balm
28 SILPHIUM PERFOLIATUM
  Cup Plant
29 ACONITUM CARMICHAELII
  Monkshood
30 POLYSTICHUM ACROSTICHOIDES
  Christmas Fern
31 OSMUNDA CINNAMOMEA
  Cinnamon Fern

MISCELLANEOUS

32 EXISTING TREES
33 ENTRY DRIVE
34 DRIVE TO GUEST HOUSE
35 SEPTIC FIELD
36 SCULPTURE
37 STONE-PAVED PATH
38 WOODLAND

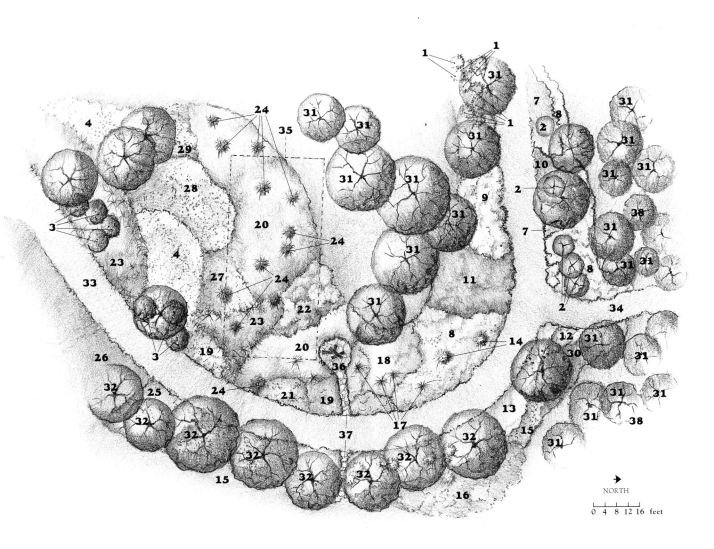

Instead of lawn, layers of perennials and shrubs sweep across the front of the house. The palette includes Panicum virgatum with its smoky bloom in summer and the soft yellow flowers of Helianthus angustifolius (swamp sunflower).
Richard Felber photograph

We thought our garden would be static, but it's always in motion. The grasses, moving in the wind, are very romantic. I paint with watercolor, so I use the garden as a palette, moving things around for balance, texture, and color.

—GRETCHEN FELDMAN

Wolfgang is a bit of a genius in his foresight, resulting in a garden that is like a kaleidoscope. He visualized what the garden would look like in each season. It is especially beautiful in winter. Recently we were there during a wet snow, and the garden was spectacular, actually glistening.

—SAMUEL FELDMAN

THE FELDMAN GARDEN

Nature set the theme for this rolling oceanside garden on Martha's Vineyard. A natural meadow extends from the house to the distant water's edge, and subtle topography creates foreground views that compete for attention. Occasional glimpses of meandering inlets complete the compelling image of land meeting water. The exquisite design of the Feldmans' vacation house complements the total composition. Its simple lines, natural materials, and muted colors blend with the extraordinary surroundings. Hard surfaces in the landscape are restrained, informal, and limited to functional requirements.

The garden, which occupies the space immediately around the house, seems to flow naturally into the adjacent wild meadow and to draw the meadow's unruly beauty toward the house, framing the spectacular ocean scenery. Broad layered masses of plants help

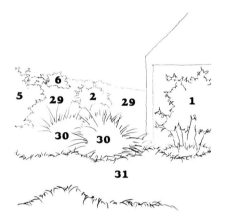

create a mature "meadow" look. A mowed grass path, invisible when viewed from the house, separates the perennial garden from the natural meadow. This path ensures that the meadow will not invade the garden, and vice versa. Boulders in the foreground tie the garden visually to the ocean's distant rocky shoreline.

When we planted the garden several years ago, we expected to find sandy island soil but found clay instead. We replaced the top twelve inches with topsoil and amended it with Milorganite and fish emulsion. We chose the plants carefully for seaside conditions. They are resistant to salt spray and heavy ocean winds. Although we included an automatic irrigation system, the plants are also drought resistant. The result is like a xeric landscape, in that it does well with very little moisture.

The garden attracts wildlife, such as raccoons, skunks, and the ever-present deer. The Feldmans have tried everything to hold the deer at bay, including rotten eggs and an electric fence. Although this puts them off temporarily, the garden is constantly threatened by their appetites and antics. In spite of their vigilance, the Feldmans find fresh hoofprints around the garden almost every morning.

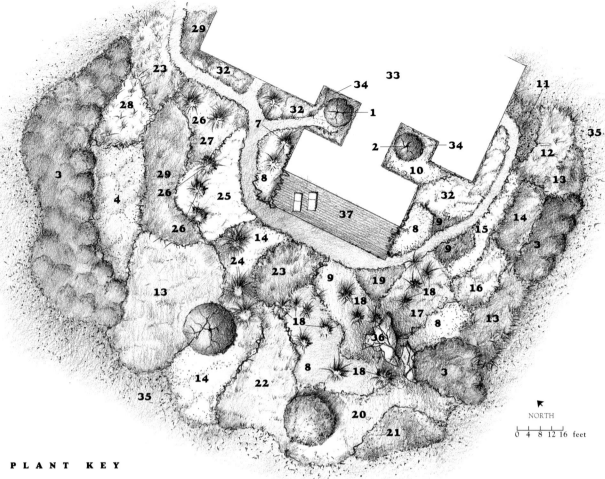

PLANT KEY

TREES AND SHRUBS

1 MAGNOLIA VIRGINIANA
Sweet Bay Magnolia

2 AMELANCHIER CANADENSIS
Shadblow Serviceberry

3 VIBURNUM SPP.
Viburum

4 CYTISUS X PRAECOX
Warminster Broom

5 HAMAMELIS MOLLIS 'BREVIPETALA'
Chinese Witch Hazel

6 PINUS THUNBERGIANA
Japanese Black Pine

PERENNIALS AND ORNAMENTAL GRASSES

7 MISCANTHUS SINENSIS 'YAKU JIMA'
Silver Grass

8 PEROVSKIA ATRIPLICIFOLIA
Russian Sage

9 MOLINIA LITORIALIS 'KARL FOERSTER'
Purple Moor Grass

10 COREOPSIS VERTICILLATA 'MOONBEAM'
Cutleaf Tickseed

11 SALVIA NEMOROSA 'MAINACHT'
Sage

12 MISCANTHUS SINENSIS PURPURASCENS
Red Maiden Grass

13 EUPATORIUM PURPUREUM
Joe-Pye Weed

14 SPODIOPOGON SIBIRICUS
Silver Spike Grass

15 ACHILLEA FILIPENDULINA 'CORONATION GOLD'
Coronation Gold Yarrow

16 LIATRIS SPICATA
Gayfeather

17 CHRYSANTHEMUM PACIFICUM
Gold and Silver Chrysanthemum

18 HELICTOTRICHON SEMPERVIRENS
Blue Oat Grass

19 ACANTHUS HUNGARICUS
Bear's-Breech

20 NEPETA X FAASSENII
Catnip

21 SOLIDAGO SP.
Goldenrod

22 SPARTINA PECTINATA
Prairie Cord Grass

23 PENNISETUM ORIENTALE
Oriental Fountain Grass

24 MISCANTHUS SINENSIS 'GRACILLIMUS'
Japanese Silver Grass

25 SEDUM X 'RUBY GLOW'
Stonecrop

26 MISCANTHUS SINENSIS 'CONDENSATUS'
Japanese Silver Grass

27 ARTEMISIA SP.
Wormwood

28 PENNISETUM ALOPECUROIDES
Fountain Grass

29 PANICUM VIRGATUM 'HAENSE HERMS'
Red Switch Grass

30 IRIS SIBIRICA
Siberian Iris

31 LIRIOPE MUSCARI 'BIG BLUE'
Lily-Turf

32 SEDUM X 'AUTUMN JOY'
Stonecrop

MISCELLANEOUS

33 RESIDENCE

34 COURTYARD

35 MEADOW

36 ROCK OUTCROPPING

37 DECK

The Feldmans maintain their garden scrupulously themselves, with some part-time help. "I'm a restless gardener," Mrs. Feldman says. "The seaside environment is hostile and requires constant vigilance. If something isn't doing well, I don't hesitate to pull it out." Mr. Feldman adds, "Wolfgang and Jim are more laissez-faire than we are. They like things wild, but if we didn't control things, we would have chaos."

Getting the garden started in the spring takes the most effort—cutting back the dried perennials, weeding, mulching, and feeding. But by the Fourth of July its spectacular beauty makes all the work worthwhile. The result is color in all four seasons.

I think the most notable quality of this planting design is the gentle transition of views that progress with increasing simplicity from the intricate perennial garden to the natural seaside meadow and, finally, to the beach and ocean in the distance.

PREVIOUS SPREAD:
In early summer, Achillea filipendulina 'Coronation Gold' sweeps right up to the edge of the deck while other perennials, shrubs, and grasses stretch to the sea (see also page 21).

LEFT: *Blue Iris sibirica (Siberian iris) blooms in early spring just as the Magnolia virginiana (sweet bay magnolia) is coming into leaf.*

OPPOSITE: *In autumn, golden dried seed heads and leaves of Miscanthus sinensis condensatus (purple blooming Japanese silver grass) stand perfectly erect in a tight billowing carpet of Chrysanthemum pacificum.*
RICHARD FELBER PHOTOGRAPHS

ROGER FOLEY

F rancis Scott Key Park honors the author of the words to "The Star-Spangled Banner," our national anthem. The prominent site, in close proximity to Key's home at the time he wrote the anthem, commands dramatic views of the Potomac River, the Georgetown waterfront, and many of Washington's notable build-

FRANCIS SCOTT KEY PARK

ings and historic landmarks. One edge of the park descends in a steep slope to the Chesapeake and Ohio Canal National Historical Park. The historic Key Bridge, an important gateway to the District of Columbia from Virginia, borders the park on the west.

Wolfgang and I seldom encounter projects with so many competing influences. We had to satisfy a design program that called for dramatic combinations of landscaping, architecture, and sculpture, while respecting the site's history, natural features, and location. We knew immediately that a powerful planting scheme would be required to reconcile all the competing forces.

A circular arbor covered with *Wisteria floribunda* 'Ivory Tower' (Japanese wisteria) is the centerpiece of our design. It focuses at-

tention on a bronze bust of Francis Scott Key by the sculptor Betty Mailhouse Dunston. Nearby, we created a central greensward where a lighted fifteen-star, fifteen-stripe flag flies day and night. It is a replica of the one that inspired the anthem, which flew over Fort McHenry in Baltimore during the bombing by the British in 1814.

Gentle terraces of lush meadowlike plantings descend the park's sloping edge to the canal. "Seatwalls" set into the planted slopes invite visitors to rest in the midst of the busy city and to reflect on the history and significance of the place.

The planting plan includes more than 7,000 colorful perennials and 32,000 bulbs, as well as many flowering trees and shrubs. The plant palette includes *Cercidiphyllum japonicum* (katsura tree), *Sophora japonica* 'Regent' (Japanese pagoda tree), *Rosa* 'Pink Meidiland', *Hamamelis* x *intermedia* 'Arnold Promise' (witch hazel), *Cornus mas* (cornelian cherry), *Buddleia davidii* 'Nanho Purple' (butterfly bush), *Cotoneaster salicifolius* (willowleaf cotoneaster), *Panicum virgatum, Pennisetum alopecuroides,* and *Hemerocallis* spp. (daylily).

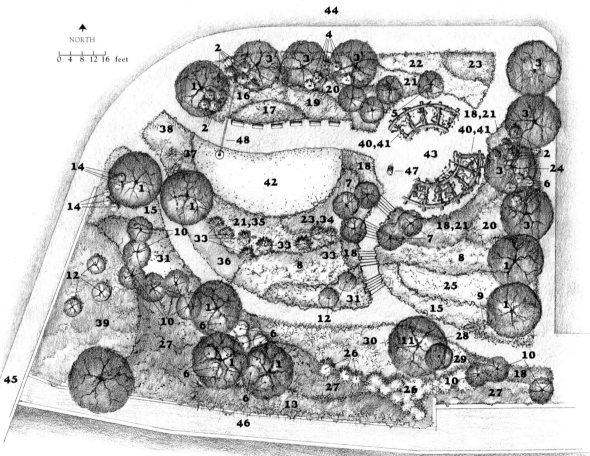

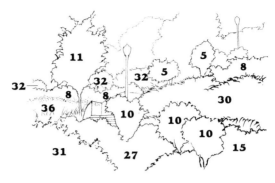

PLANT KEY

TREES AND SHRUBS

1 SOPHORA JAPONICA
Japanese Pagoda Tree

2 MAHONIA AQUIFOLIUM 'COMPACTUM'
Oregon Grape Holly

3 ZELKOVA SERRATA 'HALKA'
Halka Zelkova

4 NANDINA DOMESTICA
Heavenly Bamboo

5 MAGNOLIA VIRGINIANA
Sweet Bay Magnolia

6 VIBURNUM X PRAGENSE
Prague Viburnum

7 CORNUS KOUSA
Kousa Dogwood

8 ROSA 'PINK MEIDILAND'
Pink Meidiland Rose

9 COTONEASTER SALICIFOLIUS
Willowleaf Cotoneaster

10 CORNUS MAS
Cornelian Cherry

11 CERCIDIPHYLLUM JAPONICUM
Katsura tree

12 HAMAMELIS X INTERMEDIA 'ARNOLD PROMISE'
Witch Hazel

13 FORSYTHIA X INTERMEDIA 'SPRING GLORY'
Forsythia

14 VIBURNUM SETIGERUM
Tea Viburnum

PERENNIALS AND ORNAMENTAL GRASSES

15 HYPERICUM CALYCINUM
St.-John's-Wort

16 RUDBECKIA FULGIDA 'GOLDSTURM'
Black-eyed Susan

17 VERONICA LONGIFOLIA 'SUNNY BORDER BLUE'
Blue Speedwell

18 LIRIOPE MUSCARI 'BIG BLUE'
Lily-Turf

19 MOLINIA LITORIALIS 'TRANSPARENT'
Purple Moor Grass

20 HEMEROCALLIS CITRINA
Daylily

21 PEROVSKIA ATRIPLICIFOLIA
Russian Sage

22 SEDUM X 'RUBY GLOW'
Stonecrop

23 LIATRIS SPICATA
Gayfeather

24 LIRIOPE MUSCARI 'SILVER DRAGON'
Lily-Turf

25 PENNISETUM ALOPECUROIDES
Fountain Grass

26 FARGESIA NITIDA
Blue Clump Bamboo

27 LYSIMACHIA CLETHROIDES
Gooseneck Loosestrife

28 HOSTA X 'HONEYBELLS'
Plantain Lily

29 HOSTA X 'KROSSA REGAL'
Plantain Lily

30 CALAMAGROSTIS X ACUTIFLORA STRICTA
Feather Reed Grass

31 BUDDLEIA DAVIDII
Butterfly Bush

32 MISCANTHUS SINENSIS 'SARABANDE'
Silver Grass

33 MISCANTHUS SINENSIS 'GRAZIELLA'
Japanese Maiden Grass

34 COREOPSIS VERTICILLATA 'MOONBEAM'
Cutleaf Tickseed

35 NEPETA X FAASSENII
Catnip

36 PANICUM VIRGATUM 'ROTSTRAHLBUSCH'
Red Switch Grass

37 MISCANTHUS SINENSIS 'MORNING LIGHT'
Silver Grass

38 MISCANTHUS SINENSIS PURPURASCENS
Red Maiden Grass

39 LAMIUM GALEOBDOLON
Yellow Archangel

VINES (ON ARBOR)

40 WISTERIA FLORIBUNDA 'IVORY TOWER'
Japanese Wisteria

41 WISTERIA FLORIBUNDA 'PLENA'
Japanese Wisteria

MISCELLANEOUS

42 LAWN

43 ARBOR

44 M STREET

45 KEY BRIDGE

46 TOW PATH

47 STATUE

48 FLAG POLE

THE GRATZ GARDEN

*I wanted a naturalistic landscape; the kind I grew up with
in the fields and woods of North Carolina.*

—JACQUELINE GRATZ

*Not only is our garden visually appealing,
but it does all kinds of good things for us emotionally as well.*

—ERIC GRATZ

T he Gratzs' house, a large shingle-style bungalow with a classic front porch, sits
in the middle of a one-third-acre lot in a suburban Baltimore, Maryland, neighborhood that dates from the early 1900s. Mature *Pinus strobus* (eastern white
pines), several old specimens of *Picea pungens* 'Glauca' (Colorado blue spruces), and a
sculptural *Hydrangea paniculata* 'Grandiflora' (panicle hydrangea) enclose the garden
space and provide privacy.

Mrs. Gratz is an excellent gardener and plantsperson. She had definite ideas about
what she wanted in the garden and worked closely with Wolfgang on the planting design. She told him about her love for grasses and her special interests in perennials, trees,
and shrubs, especially those that attract birds. Her vegetable garden was already thriv-
ing, and she was anxious to begin a naturalistic garden.

Wolfgang chose plants that are interesting in all seasons, such as the native *Aster
novae-angliae* and *Echinacea purpurea*. "I like *Rudbeckia fulgida* 'Goldsturm', even though it
is common," Mrs. Gratz says. "I don't know which I like better, its storm of gold at the
end of summer or its chocolate-brown seedpods that attract birds all winter."

Mrs. Gratz also loves plants that bloom in early spring, such as the *Helleborus niger*
(Christmas rose), *Hamamelis mollis* 'Brevipetala' (Chinese witch hazel), and *Corylopsis pauciflora*. She has found that the *Magnolia virginiana*, a native of her home state, blooms during the summer and produces seedpods that attract birds. Warblers,
rose-breasted grosbeaks, scarlet tanagers, thrushes, and red-eyed
vireos are regular visitors. The birds also feast on *Aralia spinosa*, *Ilex
verticillata*, and *Viburnum dilatatum* (linden viburnum).

Planting day was a special treat for Mrs. Gratz. She was fascinated by Wolfgang's frenetic pace as he orchestrated the placement
of plants in her new garden. "He is just superb at that," she says. "It
makes all the difference and is key to creating a particular kind of
garden space." The result is exactly the lush garden environment
that she had envisioned (see also page xii).

ABOVE AND OPPOSITE:
ROGER FOLEY

*After the first year, the human hand disap-
peared and people no longer said, "What a great
design this is!" Design was forgotten as nature
took over. Now there are moments when I walk
around this place, looking at how land meets
water, and find in it a profound, almost religious
experience. It has brought true joy into my life.*

—CORBIN GWALTNEY

THE CORBIN AND JEAN GWALTNEY GARDEN

S oon after Wolfgang and I finished
work on the Gwaltneys' town garden in Bethesda, Maryland, they
called to tell us about a fourteen-acre property they had just purchased on the western
shore of Chesapeake Bay. They were very
pleased with the town garden and thought
the notion of planting a garden with year-
round interest would complement their new
weekend home perfectly.

They invited us to visit, and we found a
unique and spectacular property: 750 feet of
frontage on the bay, a beautifully renovated
clapboard house facing the water, a broad
lawn dappled with the shade of 125-year-
old *Quercus albas* (white oaks), and a perime-

*This planting area, shown here in spring, is the same as that
shown in autumn on page 60. Thousands of spring-blooming narcissus are planted between the perennials and grasses in October.
The bulbs have naturalized and bloom year after year.*

ter frame of dense woods. We knew immediately that the garden's design would require great restraint. Our job was to enhance the site's natural beauty, not to compete with it.

We overcame many obstacles to achieve the garden's relaxed and easy look. The soil was heavy and alternately flooded and parched; it had to be amended before planting. Tree root systems are very shallow because of the high, brackish water table; planting beds had to be elevated for new trees and shrubs. High winds and salt spray from occasional severe storms dictated our selection of tough plants that would tolerate wind, flood, and drought. Happily, our plants take wind in stride. According to an old Arab proverb, "Grasses dance in the wind and lie down in the storm."

By adjusting the shape of the lawn our planting plan directs even more attention to the panorama of sky and water. We contained the lawn within a broad border of plants that we selected from a natural palette and laid out on an exaggerated scale. The result is a harmonious progression of layers from the lawn to the lush ornamental garden and, finally, to the forest in the background.

Giant swaths of waist-high plants make up the ornamental garden. The plant list includes *Pennisetum alopecuroides, Petasites japonicus* (Japanese butterbur), *Hemerocallis citrina* (daylily), *Calamagrostis acutiflora stricta, Panicum virgatum, Kalmia latifolia* (mountain laurel), *Amelanchier canadensis* (shadblow serviceberry), *Hosta sieboldiana, Astilbe* spp. (false spirea), *Chrysanthemum pacificum,* and *Cornus kousa* (kousa dogwood). Considering the expansive planting areas, we used relatively few plant species. For example, in one 6,000-square-foot segment of the garden, only twelve species are represented. Restraint is the key to this garden's pleasing scale and luxuriant beauty.

The Gwaltney garden is charming year-round. Spring-blooming bulbs herald the growing season—we planted 120,000 the first year and about 20,000 a year since then. In summer the place takes on a tropical look, and in winter it resembles a giant arrangement of dried foliage.

The garden creates the impression of a great outdoor living room—genteel, but a little wild around the edges. Even the surrounding wilderness is carefully controlled to give the effect of untamed, reckless nature. "The orchestrations of light, texture, and form seem suited to the pastoral waterside setting. [The style] performs the ulterior role of balancing the earth-bound energy of the meadow with the dynamic beauty of the Chesapeake Bay," wrote Adrian Higgins in *Landscape Architecture* in October 1992. Mr. Gwaltney says, "This garden and my earlier town garden show how a client and designer can form a good relationship and produce a result that neither could have created on their own."

Opposite and Above: The planting area, seen here from two directions in summer, is lush with bold stripes of Hemerocallis spp. (day lily) in deep red and lemon yellow, blue-gray foliage of Rudbeckia maxima, mauve Eupatorium purpureum (joe-pye weed) blossoms, and giant platelike leaves of Petasites japonicus (Japanese butterbur).

Right: After the perennials and grasses are cut down close to the ground in early spring, the garden is briefly open and stark looking. Notice the spot of color at the edge of the deck where spring-blooming bulbs are planted in pots.

PLANT KEY

TREES AND SHRUBS

1   ACER RUBRUM
Red Maple

2   ILEX GLABRA 'DENSA'
Inkberry Holly

3   ILEX VERTICILLATA 'SPARKLEBERRY'
Winterberry Holly

4   ILEX OPACA
American Holly

5   NYSSA SYLVATICA
Black Gum

6   MYRICA CERIFERA
Southern Wax-Myrtle

7   MAGNOLIA VIRGINIANA 'AUSTRALIS'
Sweet Bay Magnolia

8   ILEX X MESERVEAE 'BLUE STALLION'
Meserve Holly

9   RHODODENDRON X 'DELAWARE
VALLEY WHITE'
White Azalea

10   EUONYMUS KIAUTSCHOVICUS
'MANHATTAN'
Euonymus

PERENNIALS AND ORNAMENTAL
GRASSES

11   MISCANTHUS SINENSIS GIGANTEUS
Giant Chinese Silver Grass

12   LYTHRUM SALICARIA 'MORDEN'S
PINK'
Loosestrife

13   GERANIUM MACRORRHIZUM
Bigroot Geranium

14   PHYSOSTEGIA VIRGINIANA 'VIVID'
False Dragonhead

15   HIBISCUS MOSCHEUTOS 'MIXED
COLORS'
Rose Mallow

16   RUDBECKIA MAXIMA
Great Cone Flower

17   BOLTONIA ASTEROIDES 'SNOWBANK'
White Boltonia

18   MOLINIA LITORIALIS 'TRANSPARENT'
Purple Moor Grass

19   PELTIPHYLLUM PELTATUM
Umbrella Plant

20   MISCANTHUS SINENSIS 'MALEPARTUS'
Silver Grass

21   CARYOPTERIS X CLANDONENSIS
'BLUEMIST'
Bluebeard

22   CALAMAGROSTIS ACUTIFLORA STRICTA
Feather Reed Grass

23   PENNISETUM ALOPECUROIDES
'MOUDRY'
Fountain Grass

24   LYSIMACHIA CLETHROIDES
Gooseneck Loosestrife

25   CHELONE LYONII
Turtle-Head

26   HOSTA X 'HONEYBELLS'
Plantain Lily

27   LIGULARIA DENTATA 'DESDEMONA'
Goldenray

28   FERNS (MIXED SPECIES)

29   ANEMONE JAPONICA 'WHIRLWIND'
White Japanese Anemone

30   ASTILBE TAQUETII 'SUPERBA'
Purple Rose Astilbe

31   ASTILBE JAPONICA 'DEUTSCHLAND'
White False Spiraea

32   HEMEROCALLIS CITRINA
Daylily

33   HEMEROCALLIS 'STELLA D'ORO'
Daylily

34   MISCANTHUS SINENSIS 'GRACILLIMUS'
Japanese Maiden Grass

35   HOSTA VENTRICOSA 'AUREO-
MARGINATA'
Plantain Lily

36   HOSTA SIEBOLDIANA
Plantain Lily

37   VERNONIA NOVEBORACENSIS
New York Ironweed

38   ACHILLEA FILIPENDULINA
Yarrow

39   PENNISETUM ALOPECUROIDES
Fountain Grass

40   STOKESIA LAEVIS 'BLUE DANUBE'
Blue Stokesia

41   SESLERIA AUTUMNALIS
Autumn Moor Grass

42   LIRIOPE MUSCARI 'BIG BLUE'
Lily-Turf

43   PANICUM VIRGATUM 'HAENSE HERMS'
Red Switch Grass

44   ASTER MACROPHYLLUS 'ALBUS'
Bigleaf Aster

45   PETASITES JAPONICUS
Butterbur

46   ACANTHUS HUNGARICUS
Bear's-Breech

47   IMPERATA CYLINDRICA 'RED BARON'
Japanese Blood Grass

48   VERONICA LONGIFOLIA
'SUNNY BORDER BLUE'
Blue Speedwell

49   RUDBECKIA FULGIDA 'GOLDSTURM'
Black-eyed Susan

50   CHRYSANTHEMUM PACIFICUM
*Gold and Silver
chrysanthemum*

51   SEDUM X 'RUBY GLOW'
Stonecrop

52   BRUNNERA MACROPHYLLA
Siberian Bugloss

53   LYTHRUM SALICARIA 'STICHFLAMME'
European Red Loosestrife

54   IRIS SIBIRICA 'CAESAR'S BROTHER'
Siberian Iris

MISCELLANEOUS

55   RESIDENCE

56   HERB GARDEN, VEGETABLE GARDEN,
CUTTING GARDEN

57   LAWN

58   TENNIS COURT

59   WOODLAND EDGE

60   GUEST HOUSE

61   POOL AND POOL DECK

62   BENCH

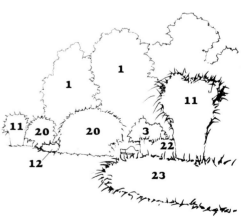

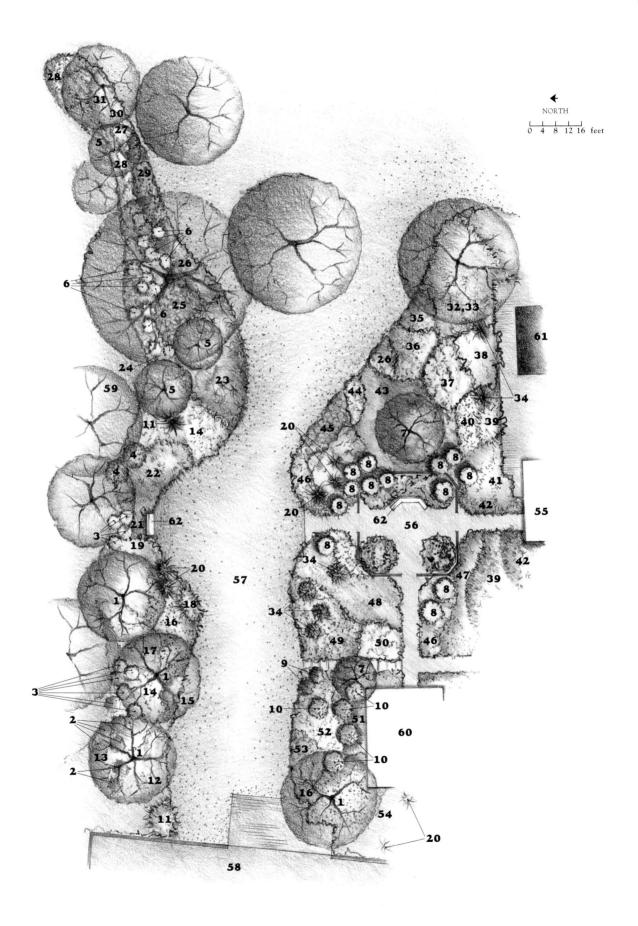

NORTH

0 4 8 12 16 feet

I love it here! I can look out my windows from any room in the house and there's a vista—even from the bedroom. I never close the shades because I have this wonderful view of nature.

—CYNTHIA HAMOWY

This two-and-a-half-acre garden and 1960s ranch-style house are a short distance from Long Island's Atlantic Ocean shoreline in Bridgehampton, New York. Few improvements had been made to the property, so we started the design with a "clean slate." This is our favorite situation, but one that seldom occurs. The Hamowys

THE HAMOWY GARDEN

did very little to the outside of the house, except for painting the red brick white. The otherwise undistinguished house now "zings," according to Mrs. Hamowy, because of beautiful plantings that sweep right up to the outside walls.

We approached the planting design like a painter approaches a canvas. Our "canvas" was the flat surface around the house, and our media were clusters of trees, shrubs, perennials, and lawn. Like the artist working with a broad brush, we planted overlapping fields of color and texture. The bold patterns and three-dimensional qualities of the planting add interest to the level site and screen unwanted views of neighboring properties.

Red and white Astilbe sp. (false spirea), a blue backdrop of Picea pungens 'Glauca' (Colorado blue spruce), and dramatic contrasts in leaf textures and plant heights give this part of the garden great panache.
RICHARD FELBER PHOTOGRAPH

BELOW: Rudbeckia maxima *steals the show in summer while* Arundo donax variegata *(striped giant reed) adds just the right sculptural touch.*

OPPOSITE: *The efflorescence of* Molinia caerulea arundinacea *is like a fire in the center of the circular driveway. Shown here in the low autumn sun, it is framed between an* Acer pseudoplatanus *(rock maple) overhead and dried seed heads of* Hosta spp. *(plantain lily),* Astilbe sp. *(false spirea), and* Hemerocallis spp. *(daylily) leaves at the ground plane.*

BELOW, RIGHT, AND OPPOSITE: RICHARD FELBER PHOTOGRAPHS

Mrs. Hamowy expressed definite ideas about the color palette for the back garden. She wanted a rich blend of purple, blue, silver, and fuchsia. We listened to her preferences and responded with a mix of *Hibiscus moscheutos* 'Anne Arundel' (rose mallow), *Panicum virgatum* 'Heavy Metal', *Monarda didyma* 'Purpurkrome' (purple bee balm), and *Miscanthus sinensis* 'Rotsilber'.

The edges of a free-form lawn define planting areas in both front and back. The back lawn acts as a foil for lush plant masses and provides convenient access to the tennis court. We treated the lawn itself as a tapestry; the maintenance pattern transitions from conventional mowing near the center to rough mowing at the edges and, finally, to natural meadow near the property line. The mowing schedule varies accordingly: once a week for the center, once a month for the edges, and once a year

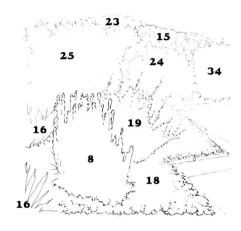

for the meadow. Mrs. Hamowy likes what she describes as "the rough and wild look at the edges."

The unfolding of elements in the Hamowy garden meets my goal for a successful design. Immediately upon arrival one is immersed in beautiful planting, while the house remains almost unseen. Slowly the constructed parts of the garden emerge—beautifully crafted "bones" that support the planting. Finally, upon entering the house, the full glory of the garden is revealed through expansive glass walls, windows, and doors. In effect, the house becomes a viewing platform for the garden's many components, both front and back (see also page 19).

PLANT KEY

TREES AND SHRUBS

1   BETULA NIGRA 'HERITAGE'
    River Birch
2   MAACKIA AMURENSIS
    Amur Maackia
3   BUDDLEIA DAVIDII
    Butterfly Bush
4   PICEA GLAUCA
    White Spruce
5   VIBURNUM SETIGERUM
    Tea Viburnum
6   HYDRANGEA QUERCIFOLIA
    Oakleaf Hydrangea

PERENNIALS AND ORNAMENTAL GRASSES

7   LIRIOPE MUSCARI 'BIG BLUE'
    Lily-Turf
8   LIATRIS SPICATA
    Gayfeather
9   ACANTHUS HUNGARICUS
    Bear's-Breech
10 FARGESIA NITIDA
    Blue Clump Bamboo
11 HYPERICUM CALYCINUM
    St.-John's-Wort
12 SEDUM X 'AUTUMN JOY'
    Stonecrop
13 SPODIOPOGON SIBIRICUS
    Silver Spike Grass

14 MONARDA DIDYMA 'PURPURKRONE'
    Purple Bee Balm
15 MISCANTHUS SINENSIS 'GRACILLIMUS'
    Japanese Maiden Grass
16 YUCCA FILAMENTOSA
    Adam's Needle
17 PANICUM VIRGATUM 'HEAVY METAL'
    Switch Grass
18 COREOPSIS VERTICILLATA 'MOONBEAM'
    Cutleaf Tickseed
19 PEROVSKIA ATRIPLICIFOLIA
    Russian Sage
20 PENNISETUM ALOPECUROIDES
    Fountain Grass
21 EUPATORIUM PURPUREUM
    Joe-Pye Weed
22 MISCANTHUS SINENSIS 'ROTSILBER'
    Chinese Silver Grass
23 RUDBECKIA MAXIMA
    Great Cone Flower
24 LYTHRUM SALICARIA 'MORDEN'S PINK'
    Loosestrife
25 CALAMAGROSTIS ACUTIFLORA STRICTA
    Feather Reed Grass
26 HIBISCUS MOSCHEUTOS 'ANNE ARUNDEL'
    Pink Rose Mallow
27 MOLINIA CAERULEA ARUNDINACEA 'WINDSPIEL'
    Tall Purple Moor Grass
28 NEPETA X FAASSENII
    Catnip

29 CHRYSANTHEMUM PACIFICUM
    Gold and Silver Chrysanthemum
30 CARYOPTERIS X CLANDONENSIS 'DARK KNIGHT'
    Bluebeard
31 NEPETA SIBIRICA
    Catmint
32 MISCANTHUS SINENSIS GIGANTEUS
    Giant Chinese Silver Grass
33 ASTER X FRIKARTII 'MÖNCH'
    Hardy Purple Aster
34 EUPHORBIA PALUSTRIS
    Spurge

MISCELLANEOUS

35 RESIDENCE
36 POOL HOUSE
37 SWIMMING POOL
38 TERRACE
39 TENNIS COURT
40 HOT TUB
41 ROUGH LAWN
42 LAWN

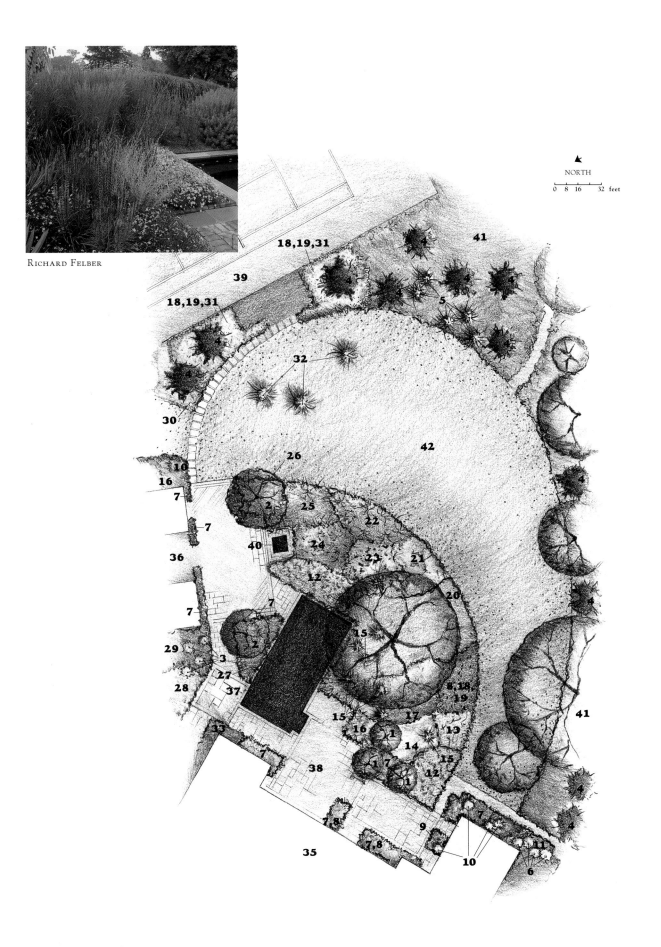

RICHARD FELBER

NORTH

0 8 16 32 feet

18,19,31

39

18,19,31

41

4

4

5

4

32

30

42

10

16

26

7

2

25

7

22

40

4

24

36

23

21

7

12

20

7

2

15

29

3

8,18,19

27

28

37

17

33

15

13

16

1

41

14

38

1 7

15

1

12

7,8

9

7

7,8

10

35

11

10

6

THE HELMS GARDEN

*We were innovators in 1978. Now many of our neighbors are
taking out their lawns too. I think, coming from England as I do,
if you can't have a good lawn, it's better to do without.*

—CYNTHIA HELMS

When we first studied the Helmses' Washington, D.C., property in 1978 it was heavily shaded by many specimens of *Ulmus americana* (American elm). Fortunately, these magnificent trees have not been affected by Dutch elm disease and are still standing. We also found that, as is typical of many older suburban houses, the shrubs planted next to the house had grown out of control and were covering up the windows. A dense border of *Rhododendron* spp. (azaleas) and *Taxus cuspidata* (Japanese yews) almost completely obscured the house.

We moved the *Rhododendron* spp. from the front of the house to the property line, where it defines the garden boundary and provides privacy from the neighbors. The Helmses were out of town on the day we moved the shrubs, and we wondered if it was deliberate. But upon return they were pleased and surprised to find their newly exposed house to be quite attractive.

A successful lawn is impossible in a densely shaded space. The Helmses' lawn was so deep in the shade that we convinced them to remove it entirely. Then we planted the entire ground plane with a collection of shade-loving plants, including *Adiantum pedatum* (maidenhair fern), *Epimedium* spp. (barrenwort), *Hosta* spp. (plantain lily), *Ligularia dentata* 'Desdemona', *Liriope muscari* 'Big Blue' (lily-turf), and *Lamium galeobdolon* (yellow archangel). Four *Ilex* x *attenuata* 'Fosteri' (Foster holly) and one *Ilex opaca* (American holly) were placed close to the curb to soften the view of street traffic. The *Ilex opaca* becomes the Helmses' Christmas tree when it is decorated with lights during the holiday season—a special treat for the grandchildren. *Hamamelis* x *intermedia* 'Arnold Promise' (witch hazel) and *Fargesia nitida* complete the composition and provide sculptural interest.

Mrs. Helms laughs about having "conversations" with her plants. "If they aren't doing well," she says, "I talk it over with them and give them one more chance." She must be doing the right thing, for her garden has been a great success over the years. In fact, it has influenced the neighborhood. When the garden was first planted, skeptical neighbors viewed it as extreme, and gossiped about their peculiar decision to remove the lawn. But now many neighbors have replaced their lawns with perennial "meadows."

This large front garden stands in lush contrast to its typical suburban neighbors in Winchester, Virginia. Its unusual topography accentuates its appeal: the entrance to the house is several feet below street level, and the driveway descends from the street in a gentle curve toward the house, terminating in a generous circle next to the front door. A walled garden adjacent to the entrance extends from the kitchen. We inherited mature trees that tower overhead as well as several Colorado blue spruces (*Picea pungens* 'Glauca') from a previous design.

THE WENDELL AND DOROTHY HESTER GARDEN

Mr. Hester envisioned the front garden as a place for Mrs. Hester to actively enjoy. He wanted very little lawn—just enough to show respect for the vernacular of the neighborhood—and asked instead for lush plantings and a rambling network of walking paths. To this we added benches from which visitors can enjoy the Hesters' delightful private park.

We transplanted the *Picea pungens* 'Glauca' specimens along the property line to make them less obvious. Now they provide privacy and act as a backdrop for the perennial garden. Although

PLANT KEY

TREES AND SHRUBS

1 ZELKOVA SERRATA
 Japanese Zelkova
2 CLADRASTIS LUTEA
 American Yellowwood
3 ILEX X 'NELLIE R. STEVENS'
 Nellie R. Stevens Holly
4 ILEX VERTICILLATA 'SPARKLEBERRY'
 Winterberry Holly
5 PINUS BUNGEANA
 Lacebark Pine
6 PICEA PUNGENS 'GLAUCA'
 Colorado Spruce
7 AMELANCHIER CANADENSIS
 Shadblow Serviceberry
8 MAHONIA BEALII
 Leatherleaf Mahonia
9 MAGNOLIA STELLATA
 Star Magnolia
10 CORYLOPSIS PAUCIFLORA
 Buttercup Winter Hazel
11 RHODODENDRON MAXIMUM
 Rosebay Rhododendron
12 HAMAMELIS X INTERMEDIA 'ARNOLD
 PROMISE'
 Witch Hazel
13 VIBURNUM PRUNIFOLIUM
 Black Haw Viburnum
14 CORNUS MAS
 Cornelian Cherry
15 CORNUS KOUSA
 Kousa Dogwood
16 SOPHORA JAPONICA
 Japanese Pagoda Tree
17 LAGERSTROEMIA INDICA
 Crape Myrtle

PERENNIALS AND ORNAMENTAL GRASSES

18 SPODIOPOGON SIBIRICUS
 Silver Spike Grass
19 RUDBECKIA FULGIDA 'GOLDSTURM'
 Black-eyed Susan
20 SEDUM X 'WEIHENSTEPHANER GOLD'
 Stonecrop
21 ASTER X FRIKARTII 'MÖNCH'
 Hardy Purple Aster
22 AGAPANTHUS UMBELLATUS 'BLUE
 TRIUMPHATOR'
 Lily of the Nile
23 LIRIOPE MUSCARI 'BIG BLUE'
 Lily-Turf

24 SALVIA NEMOROSA 'MAINACHT'
 Sage
25 SESLERIA AUTUMNALIS
 Autumn Moor Grass
26 PHLOMIS SAMIA
 Greek Sage
27 MISCANTHUS SINENSIS PURPURASCENS
 Red Maiden Grass
28 CAREX MORROWII VARIEGATA
 Variegated Japanese Sedge
29 EPIMEDIUM SPP.
 Barrenwort
30 BERGENIA CORDIFOLIA
 Heartleaf Bergenia
31 FERNS (MIXED SPECIES)
32 FARGESIA NITIDA
 Blue Clump Bamboo
33 ANEMONE HUPEHENSIS 'SEPTEMBER
 CHARM'
 Pink Japanese Anemone
34 LIGULARIA DENTATA 'DESDEMONA'
 Goldenray
35 BRUNNERA MACROPHYLLA
 Siberian Bugloss
36 ASTILBE SPP.
 False Spiraea
37 CIMICIFUGA RACEMOSA
 Black Snakeroot
38 BEGONIA GRANDIS
 Hardy Pink Begonia
39 HEMEROCALLIS 'STELLA D'ORO'
 Daylily
40 ARALIA RACEMOSA
 Spikenard
41 HOSTA X 'HONEYBELLS'
 Plantain Lily
42 GERANIUM GRANDIFLORUM
 Cranesbill
43 ACANTHUS HUNGARICUS
 Bear's-Breech
44 PANICUM VIRGATUM 'HAENSE HERMS'
 Red Switch Grass
45 ACHILLEA FILIPENDULINA
 'CORONATION GOLD'
 Yarrow
46 PEROVSKIA ATRIPLICIFOLIA
 Russian Sage
47 BOLTONIA ASTEROIDES
 Boltonia

MISCELLANEOUS

48 RESIDENCE
49 ENTRY COURT
50 LAWN

FOLLOWING SPREAD: Autumn's dried bouquet consists of chocolate-brown seed heads of Rudbeckia fulgida 'Goldsturm', golden leaves of Spodiopogon sibiricus, evergreen canes of Fargesia nitida, and the bony structure of Hamamelis x intermedia 'Arnold Promise' (witch hazel). The blue backdrop is Picea pungens 'Glauca' (Colorado blue spruce).

we wouldn't normally choose an alpine plant for Virginia, the blue color and fine texture of the *Picea pungens* 'Glauca' provide a jazzy background for the oranges, yellows, and reds we planted in the foreground. The plant list includes *Imperata cylindrica* 'Red Baron' (Japanese blood grass), *Hemerocallis* spp. (daylily), *Boltonia asteroides* 'Snowbank', *Bergenia cordifolia* (heartleaf bergenia), *Begonia grandis* (hardy pink begonia), and *Aster novae-angliae* 'Alma Poetschke'. We planted this palette in masses under a canopy of *Quercus albas* (white oaks).

The Hesters' front garden is like a vast collage that changes color and scale throughout the year. Thanks to its perfect tilt, it can be seen to advantage from many rooms in the house.

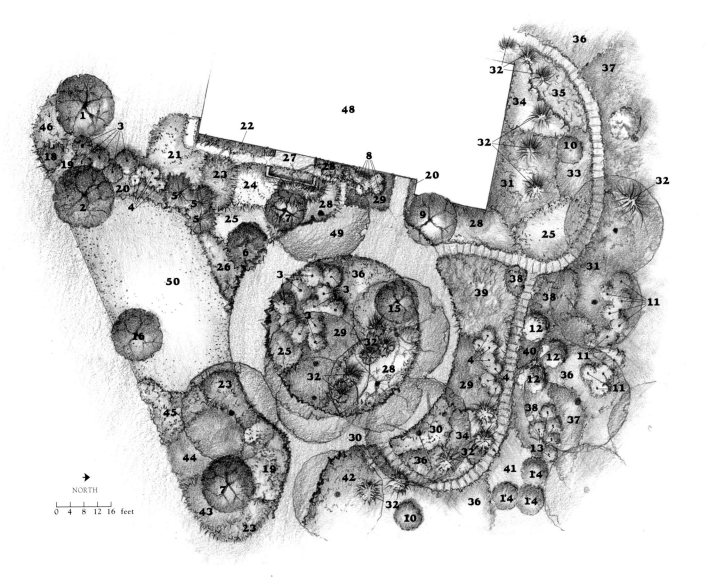

NORTH

0 4 8 12 16 feet

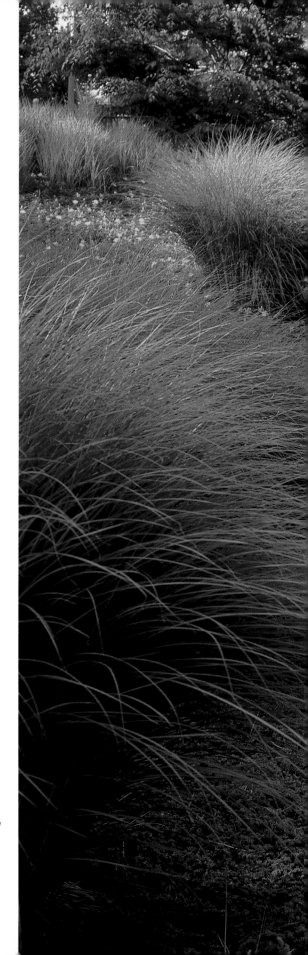

> *The two public parks at the International Center are among Washington's best-kept secrets. There's a major park in the center of the complex and an intimate garden just north of the Austrian Chancery. Both are eye-poppingly beautiful.*
>
> —BENJAMIN FORGEY,
> *THE WASHINGTON POST*, OCTOBER 26, 1991

INTERNATIONAL CHANCERY CENTER

T he International Chancery Center is located in a highly urban community setting. The United States Department of State decided to transform this twenty-eight-acre property in northwest Washington, D.C., into a prestigious community of twenty-two international diplomatic missions and the headquarters of the International Telecommunications Satellite Organization (INTELSAT). Originally designed and constructed in the mid-1980s, the International Chancery Center is already home to INTELSAT, a federal office building, and the chanceries of Austria, Bahrain, Egypt, Ghana, Israel, Jordan, Kuwait, and Singapore.

Our objective was to enhance each of the chancery sites by creating beautiful envelopes of planted public space around it. The sponsor agreed to dedicate all public parks, streets, and surrounding protective buffers to this effort. The result is a striking community-wide display of trees, grasses, perennials, and bulbs, mingled with established woodlands.

Juniperus squamata 'Blue Carpet' *(blue carpet juniper) and* Hypericum calycinum *stabilize this steep bank while sculptural clumps of* Miscanthus sinensis 'Gracillimus' *and a delicate canopy of* Sophora japonica *(Japanese pagoda tree) add vertical interest and layering.*

RICHARD FELBER

The slope shown above in spring with 700,000
Narcissus sp. in bloom is the same as that shown on
the right in summer.
VOLKMAR WENTZEL PHOTOGRAPH

A two-acre central park occupies the apex of this rolling site. It is a lushly planted haven where employees and neighbors gather. Walkways and steps lead visitors through drifts of *Hemerocallis* spp. (daylily), *Juniperus squamata* 'Blue Carpet' (blue carpet juniper), *Tanacetum macrophyllum, Lysimachia clethroides* (gooseneck loosestrife), *Helleborous* sp. (lenten rose), and *Tiarella cordifolia*. Plants spill out of the park and continue along streetscapes throughout the community. Steep wooded slopes at the property's edge reinforce the parklike appearance and buffer the abutting chanceries from busy thoroughfares. After selective clearing and regrading, we enhanced these natural buffers with masses of erosion-control plantings. Finally, we disguised a required storm-water retention basin in the northwest corner of the property as a quiet sunken garden, shaded by *Taxodium distichum* (bald cypress). This garden is a favorite respite for neighborhood residents, many of whom once expressed apprehension about the project but now use it as an extension of their own front yards.

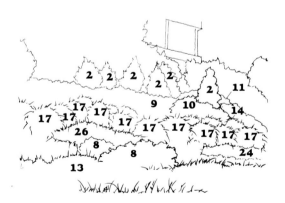

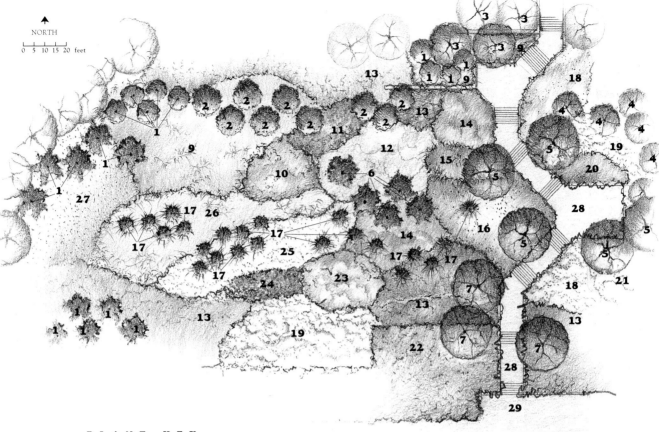

NORTH

0 5 10 15 20 feet

PLANT KEY

TREES AND SHRUBS

1   CORNUS MAS
    Cornelian Cherry

2   ILEX X 'NELLIE R. STEVENS'
    Nellie R. Stevens Holly

3   SOPHORA JAPONICA
    Japanese Pagoda Tree

4   AMELANCHIER CANADENSIS
    Shadblow Serviceberry

5   ZELKOVA SERRATA
    Japanese Zelkova

6   PINUS THUNBERGIANA
    Japanese Black Pine

7   PYRUS CALLERYANA 'BRADFORD'
    Bradford Pear

8   EUONYMUS KIAUTSCHOVICUS
    'MANHATTAN'
    *Hybrid Spreading
    Euonymus*

PERENNIALS AND
ORNAMENTAL GRASSES

9   HEMEROCALLIS SP.
    Daylily

10 HIBISCUS MOSCHEUTOS
    Rose Mallow

11 LYTHRUM SALICARIA 'MORDEN'S
    PINK'
    Loosestrife

12 BOLTONIA ASTEROIDES 'SNOWBANK'
    White Boltonia

13 LIRIOPE MUSCARI 'BIG BLUE'
    Lily-Turf

14 PANICUM VIRGATUM 'HAENSE
    HERMS'
    Red Switch Grass

15 MISCANTHUS SINENSIS PURPURASCENS
    Red Maiden Grass

16 HYPERICUM CALYCINUM
    St.-John's-Wort

17 MISCANTHUS SINENSIS 'GRACILLIMUS'
    Japanese Maiden Grass

18 PEROVSKIA ATRIPLICIFOLIA
    Russian Sage

19 LYSIMACHIA CLETHROIDES
    Gooseneck Loosestrife

20 SPODIOPOGON SIBIRICUS
    Silver Spike Grass

21 SOLIDAGO 'GOLDENMOSA'
    Goldenrod

22 TANACETUM MACROPHYLLUM
    Tansy Daisy

23 EUPATORIUM FISTULOSUM
    'GATEWAY'
    Joe-Pye Weed

24 YUCCA FILAMENTOSA
    Adam's Needle

25 SEDUM X 'AUTUMN JOY'
    Stonecrop

26 PENNISETUM ALOPECUROIDES
    Fountain Grass

27 CAREX PENDULA
    Drooping Sedge

MISCELLANEOUS

28 STEPS

29 SIDEWALK

30 STREET

*When I help people with their gardens, it is sur-
prising to me that they don't realize that giving
birth to a garden is only the beginning and that it
will not be truly successful unless they are there to
nuture it step-by-step. They think once it's done,
it's done, but that's not how it works.*

—GAIL JACOBS

THE JACOBS
GARDEN

Lester Collins designed an earlier phase
of this two-acre garden before we
were asked to design broad planting
areas in the front and on the side of the house.
The front yard we inherited was distinguished by a riverlike ribbon of lawn bordered with many textures of foliage. We
widened existing beds on both sides of the
lawn, contained them within serpentine
edges, and planted them to overflowing with
Tiarella cordifolia, Astilbe spp. (false spirea),
Hosta spp. (plantain lily), *Epimedium perralderianum, Anemone hupehensis* (dwarf Japanese
anemone), *Begonia grandis* (hardy pink begonia), and *Carex pendula* (drooping sedge).
Shrubs include *Fargesia nitida, Ilex x attenuata*
'Fosteri' (Foster holly), and *Nandina domestica*
(heavenly bamboo). We kept the *Ilex* spp.
(hollies), *Rhododendron* spp. (azaleas), *Cornus
florida* (flowering dogwoods), and large shade
trees that existed on the site. Finally, we
planted a large *Magnolia stellata* (star magnolia)
in a place of honor at the front door.

Two bouquets arranged by Mrs. Jacobs with flowers, leaves, and fruits gathered from her summer garden (above) and fall garden (top). Courtesy of Gail L. Jacobs Flower Craft. ROGER FOLEY PHOTOGRAPHS

OPPOSITE: Hamamelis mollis 'Brevipetala' *(Chinese witch hazel) is the first to bloom in the new year. Here, its fragrant yellow flowers contrast sharply with the red berries of* Nandina domestica *(heavenly bamboo).*

The front garden is shady and quiet except for a small area at the far end where the sun breaks through. The sudden splash of distant sunlight and color surprises visitors who approach the house through a shade garden. We chose this sunny spot as the perfect place for two rectangular stone planters. By filling these bench-height beds with annuals and bulbs, Mrs. Jacobs can experiment with cut-flower arrangements.

Mrs. Jacobs plants narcissus bulbs in her perennial beds, staggering them by species for late and early bloom. She adds one thousand bulbs each year to naturalize in the woods. She plants tulips in special beds where the bulbs can be removed if they are not creating a natural cover. She doesn't like to wait for the tulip leaves to die back, so she digs up the bulbs and recycles them in the cutting beds or in the woods. As she is fond of noting, you can't count on tulips coming back. If you follow her routine, you will have beautiful tulips while they bloom, but they will not ruin the garden's natural rhythm or leave it looking messy. "I like controlled wildness—lush and overflowing," she says. "Sometimes plants get tall and leggy by midsummer, so I cut them back, and then by September they look bushy and lovely again."

Mrs. Jacobs's garden provides her with a bountiful year-round supply of materials for her work as a floral designer. She picks from the entire garden and uses the harvests to fill her house with beautiful bouquets and to demonstrate her design techniques before flower-arranging classes. Mrs. Jacobs's garden and the bouquets she creates from it honor every season. She is especially fond of fall colors, with their burgundies and pinks, and her bouquets often include grasses. Her favorite combination in the garden or in a vase is the green leaf and burgundy stem of *Ligularia dentata* 'Desdemona' and the tall blue spheres of *Allium giganteum* (giant ornamental onion).

PLANT KEY

TREES AND SHRUBS

1 RHODODENDRON SPP.
Azalea

2 ILEX X ATTENUATA 'FOSTERI'
Foster Holly

3 AMELANCHIER CANADENSIS
Shadblow Serviceberry

4 PIERIS JAPONICA
Japanese Pieris

5 HAMAMELIS MOLLIS
Chinese Witch Hazel

6 MAGNOLIA STELLATA
Star Magnolia

7 NANDINA DOMESTICA
Heavenly Bamboo

8 ILEX X 'NELLIE R. STEVENS'
Nellie R. Stevens Holly

PERENNIALS AND ORNAMENTAL GRASSES

9 LIGULARIA DENTATA 'DESDEMONA'
Goldenray

10 ASTILBE SPP.
False Spiraea

11 HOSTA X 'HONEYBELLS'
Plantain Lily

12 FERNS (MIXED SPECIES)

13 EPIMEDIUM VERSICOLOR
Barrenwort

14 BERGENIA CORDIFOLIA
Heartleaf Bergenia

15 FARGESIA NITIDA
Blue Clump Bamboo

16 BEGONIA GRANDIS
Hardy Pink Begonia

17 LIRIOPE MUSCARI 'BIG BLUE'
Lily-Turf

18 CAREX PENDULA
Drooping Sedge

19 HOSTA SIEBOLDIANA
Blue Plantain Lily

20 RODGERSIA AESCULIFOLIA
Rodgersia

21 CAREX MORROWII
Japanese Sedge

22 HOSTA VENTRICOSA
Plantain Lily

23 HEDRA HELIX
Ivy

24 GERANIUM GRANDIFLORUM 'JOHNSON'S BLUE'
Cranesbill

25 PENNISETUM ALOPECUROIDES
Fountain Grass

26 LYTHRUM SPP.
Loosestrife

27 MISCANTHUS SINENSIS PURPURASCENS
Red Maiden Grass

28 CERATOSTIGMA PLUMBAGINOIDES
Leadwort

29 CIMICIFUGA RACEMOSA
Black Snakeroot

MISCELLANEOUS

30 RESIDENCE

31 LAWN

32 RAISED BEDS FOR VEGETABLES AND CUT FLOWERS

33 DRIVEWAY

34 GATE

35 STREET

ROGER FOLEY

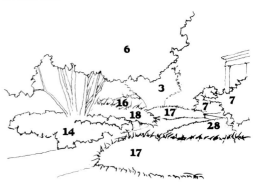

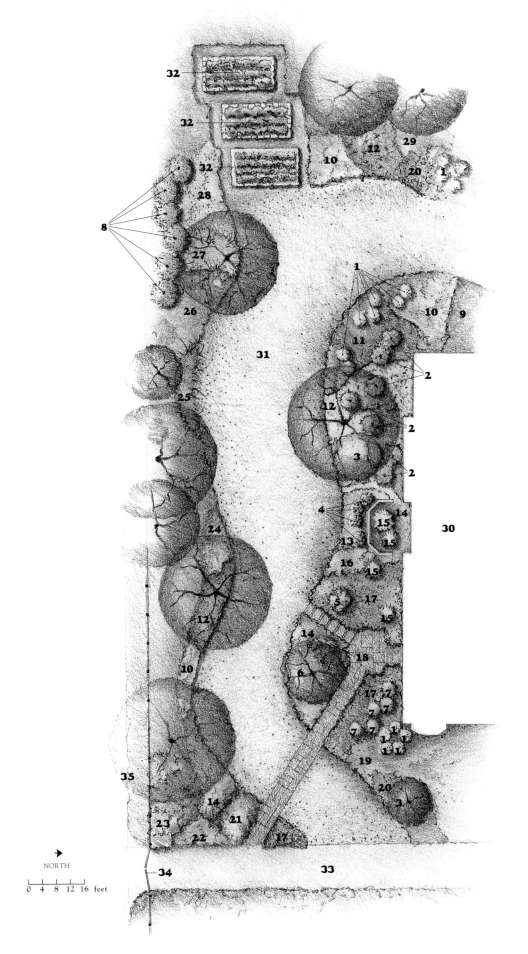

NORTH

0 4 8 12 16 feet

This suburban front garden makes a real statement. It has transformed my stodgy suburban neighborhood into a place with a touch of elegance.

—JERALD J. LITTLEFIELD

THE JERALD J. LITTLEFIELD GARDEN

This Washington, D.C., garden replaced what was once a caricature of the American suburban front yard: close-cropped lawn, an assortment of yews and hollies planted next to the house, a narrow walkway from the front door to the street, and a lone tree standing in the center of the lawn. It was a perfect opportunity to practice our philosophy that the front yard, however small, must be reclaimed for its owner's full use and enjoyment. We worked the transformation with simple tools: plants and a generously widened walkway.

The new front garden is a mini-meadow. Mounds of planting soften the edges of the realigned walkway and add three-dimensional contours to the otherwise level space. The plantings include *Sedum* x 'Autumn Joy', *Pennisetum alopecuroides*, and *Miscanthus sinensis purpurascens*. *Molinia caerulea arundinacea* 'Windspiel' provides a lacy screen of privacy at the front door, and *Ilex* x *attenuata* 'Fosteri' (Foster holly) shields the driveway. We kept the existing *Quercus palustris* (pin oak) and removed the lower branches to create a sort of umbrella over the center of the

Miscanthus sinensis purpurascens *bends under the weight of snow, while a screen of* Ilex pedunculosa *(longstalk holly) planted toward the street provides screening and just the right touch of evergreen.*

ROGER FOLEY PHOTOGRAPH

garden. We planted *Hydrangea anomala petiolaris* at the base of the tree. Now it towers over the garden to a height of about forty feet—a dramatic vertical element.

The new walkway leads to the front door, where we designed a small sitting area adjacent to the portico. It is now one of the owner's favorite places to enjoy the garden over early-morning coffee, hidden from view by lush planting.

Emulation is one measure of this garden's success. Since it was completed, about two-thirds of the front yards in the neighborhood have been replaced with rich gardens.

Notice that there is no lawn in Braque's nineteenth-century painting of a suburban
Paris house. This painting inspired me to remove the lawn in front of the Littlefield
house and to create a minimeadow in its place.(Georges Braque, The House Behind
the Trees. The Metropolitan Museum of Art, Robert Lehman Collection, 1975.
(1975.1.159). Photograph © 1992 by The Metropolitan Museum of Art.)

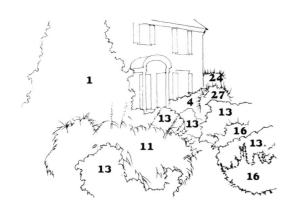

Roger Foley

PLANT KEY

TREES AND SHRUBS

1 ILEX X ATTENUATA 'FOSTERI'
Foster Holly

2 NANDINA DOMESTICA
Heavenly Bamboo

3 MAGNOLIA VIRGINIANA
Sweet Bay Magnolia

4 MAHONIA BEALII
Leatherleaf Mahonia

5 HAMAMELIS MOLLIS
Chinese Witch Hazel

6 STRANVAESIA DAVIDIANA
Chinese Stranvaesia

7 ILEX PEDUNCULOSA
Longstalk Holly

8 QUERCUS PALUSTRUS
Pin Oak

9 ILEX OPACA
American Holly

PERENNIALS AND ORNAMENTAL GRASSES

10 SEDUM X 'AUTUMN JOY'
Stonecrop

11 SPODIOPOGON SIBIRICUS
Silver Spike Grass

12 MOLINIA CAERULEA ARUNDINACEA 'WINDSPIEL'
Tall Purple Moor Grass

13 RUDBECKIA FULGIDA 'GOLDSTURM'
Black-eyed Susan

14 HIBISCUS MOSCHEUTOS
Rose Mallow

15 PENNISETUM ALOPECUROIDES
Fountain Grass

16 PEROVSKIA ATRIPLICIFOLIA
Russian Sage

17 EUPATORIUM PURPUREUM
Joe-Pye Weed

18 LIRIOPE MUSCARI 'BIG BLUE'
Big Blue Lily-Turf

19 BRUNNERA MACROPHYLLA
Siberian Bugloss

20 LIGULARIA DENTATA 'DESDEMONA'
Goldenray

21 EPIMEDIUM VERSICOLOR
Barrenwort

22 FARGESIA NITIDA
Blue Clump Bamboo

23 DESCHAMPSIA CAESPITOSA
Tufted Hair Grass

24 MISCANTHUS SINENSIS GIGANTEUS
Giant Chinese Silver Grass

25 BEGONIA GRANDIS
Hardy Pink Begonia

26 ASTILBE ARENDSII
White False Spiraea

27 MISCANTHUS SINENSIS 'GRACILLIMUS'
Japanese Maiden Grass

28 HOSTA SP.
Plantain Lily

29 SALVIA NEMOROSA 'MAINACHT'
Sage

30 MISCANTHUS SINENSIS PURPURASCENS
Red Maiden Grass

31 CARYOPTERIS X CLANDONENSIS 'BLUEMIST'
Bluebeard

32 COREOPSIS VERTICILLATA 'MOONBEAM'
Cutleaf Tickseed

33 SOLIDAGO X 'STRAHLENKRONE'
Goldenrod

MISCELLANEOUS

34 RESIDENCE

35 DRIVEWAY

36 SIDEWALK

37 FRONT WALK

38 BENCH

39 STREET

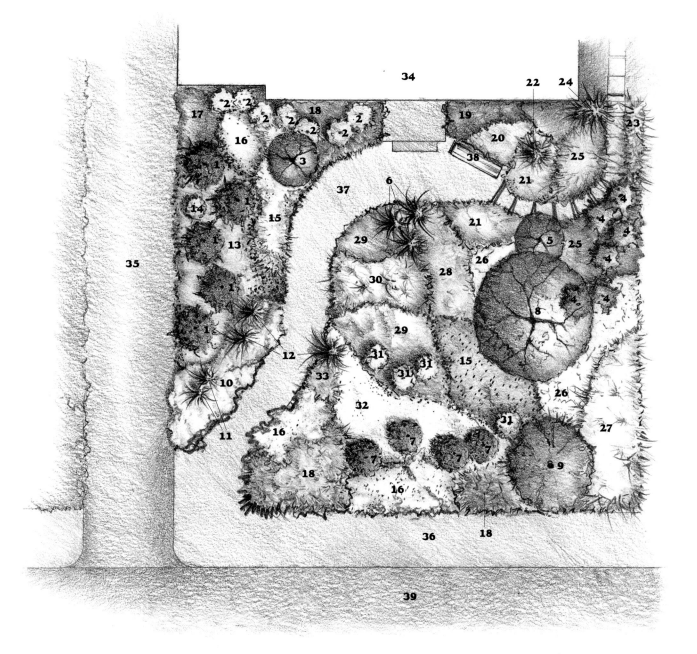

34

22 24

17 2 2 18 23

2 19

16 2 2 20 25 4

2 2 21 4

3 37 6 4

1 21 5 25

14 1 26 4

15 29 4

1 13 30 28 8 4 4

1 15

1 12 29 26 27

33 31 31

10 31 32 31

11 16 7 7

16 18 7 7 9

18 16

36 18

35

39

NORTH

0 2 4 6 8 feet

THE MARSH ESTATE GARDEN

An evergreen screen of various hollies blends gradually into the surrounding wetland forest of loblolly pine, sweetgum, red and swamp maples, and willow oaks. It is as if selected trees have simply broken with the group in the woods and wandered in to take their places in the man-made setting.

—JANE BROWN GILLETTE, LANDSCAPE ARCHITECTURE,
MARCH 1997

This is gardening with nature on the grandest scale! Nature provided the essence of the design, and man-made improvements are unobtrusive and carefully crafted. This eastern seaboard property (more than 3,000 acres) is a wonderland of lowland forests, marshes, and natural wetlands. The owner's enlightened approach added to the pleasure of the assignment. His instructions were to protect and enhance this extraordinary natural resource as an educational and recreational retreat for guests. New building on the estate has been limited to an entrance road, a lodge, a farm complex, and sports facilities.

Rustic timber stilts lift the lodge building above a tidal stream and provide sheltered spaces underneath where small boats are moored. From broad terraces and decks around the lodge one looks over a tidal pond in the foreground to lowland forests in the distance. Meandering boardwalks through the surrounding woodlands provide access to peaceful views of wetland marshes.

The natural beauty of the site inspired a straightforward planting design. We accepted the natural setting as a theme and used supplemental planting to frame views and provide foreground interest. In addition to the lodge and the farm complex, we concentrated plantings along roadways, boardwalks, hunting trails, and bridle paths. We designed these corridors as viewing platforms, from which we opened "windows" to the lodge, wetland marshes, and open ponds, where wildlife gathers.

We chose plants for their sensitivity to marsh conditions and placed them carefully to augment the natural surroundings. Because the owner spends more time at the property during the winter and spring, we emphasized plants that create more interest during those seasons. Native specimen trees include *Liquidambar styraciflua* (American sweet gum), *Ilex opaca* (American holly), *Juniperus virginiana* (eastern red cedar), and *Amelanchier canadensis* (shadblow serviceberry); shrubs include *Rhododendron periclymenoides* (pinxterbloom azalea), *Hamamelis virginiana* (common witch hazel), and *Rhus aromatica* (fragrant sumac); perennials include *Liatris spicata*, *Aster novae-angliae*, and *Solidago rugosa*; and grasses include *Panicum virgatum*, *Andropogon scoparius* (little blue stem), *Carex pendula*

(drooping sedge), and *Sorghastrum nutans*. Around ponds, drifts of water-tolerant plants such as *Lysichitom americanum* (yellow skunk cabbage), *Iris pseudacorus* (yellow flag iris), and *Hibiscus moscheutos* (rose mallow) emerge from the water's edge and creep into adjacent forests or climb embankments along roadways. We also replaced plants around buildings and in other places where they had been removed or damaged during construction.

When I first visited the Marsh Estate, I was struck by a strong sense of movement and change: the swaying of marsh grasses in the breeze, the ebb and flow of tidal streams, the busy activity of birds and other wildlife, and the playful reflections of the changing sky on the surfaces of open ponds. Even the plants showed subtle changes as they anticipated the subsequent season. As I look at the Marsh Estate Garden today, I see that nature has once more had her way and has added a final dramatic touch to the design—the unexpected richness of movement and of life.

PREVIOUS SPREAD: *The lodge resembles a bird with large flapping wings rising from a man-made pond.* Miscanthus *edges the pond in the foreground, and the wetland we reclaimed can be seen against the distant bank.*

LEFT: *The view from the lodge is framed by a rustic fence and* Cortaderia pumila *(pampas grass).*

OPPOSITE: *The teahouse is set in a landscape of* Pinus taeda *(loblolly pines) that rises from a meadow of* Panicum virgatum *and* Solidago rugosa.

THE MR. AND MRS. ULRICH MEYER GARDEN

Lake Michigan's southeastern shore is the setting for this weekend house and three-acre garden where the Meyers relax and enjoy nature, far from the workaday bustle of Chicago. The elevated site is about eighty feet above the lake and is set back three hundred feet from the water's edge. Chicago architect Michael J. Pado designed the house. Its contemporary lines and exterior stucco finish harmonize perfectly with the lakeside setting.

Our introduction to the Meyers came in a roundabout way. Wolfgang had designed a garden for Mrs. Meyer's aunt in Baltimore some thirty years earlier. Mrs. Meyer remembered the year-round beauty of her aunt's garden and envisioned a similar look for her lakeside property. Although she thought hiring designers from Washington, D.C., was extravagant, she invited us to inspect the property, and we started the design.

The assignment was delightfully nostalgic for me. As a child I had spent summers at

nearby Grand Haven Beach, where my grandparents owned a cottage. I loved splashing in the lake's fresh water, running over the grass-covered dunes, and hiking through the surrounding pine woods. Evenings meant beautiful sunsets and clear starry skies. Mrs. Meyer and I enjoy exchanging respective memories of Baltimore and Grand Haven, and our common interests influenced the garden's design. I understood the lakeside dune environment and mimicked its informal softness to achieve her image of the Baltimore garden.

Before planting, we amended the very sandy soil by rototilling a combination of mushroom soil, topsoil, and leaf mold to a depth of ten inches. Next we added *Oxydendrum arboreum* (sourwood) and *Pinus thunbergiana* (Japanese black pine) to the existing stands of *Pinus nigra* (Austrian black pine) and *Pinus sylvestris* (Scotch pine). Then came the main act: grasses of varying heights used as ground cover. They include *Panicum virgatum*, *Carex flacca* (blue-green sedge), *Miscanthus sinensis* 'Gracillimus', and *Miscanthus sinensis purpurascens*, interspersed with a lavish palette of perennials. The spectacle begins in late spring with *Achillea filipendulina* 'Coronation Gold', *Achillea millefolium* 'Red Beauty' (red yarrow), *Geranium macrorrhizum* 'Spessart', *Gaillardia* x *grandiflora* (blanket flower), and *Bergenia cordifolia* (heartleaf bergenia). As summer approaches the colors turn to the cool lavender of *Perovskia atriplicifolia*, the hot yellows of *Rudbeckia fulgida* 'Goldsturm' and *Solidago* x 'Strahlenkrone' (goldenrod), and the sparkling white of *Boltonia asteroides*. Late summer brings the soft pink of *Sedum* x 'Autumn Joy'.

A boardwalk separates the garden around the house from the natural dune and beach grasses. The boardwalk disappears in summer under overhanging plants. Also, a tennis court, which the Meyers first described to us as an "eyesore," is now completely obscured from view by a planted berm. Guests often ask, "Where is it?" The entire composition is a seamless expanse of softly billowing plant textures that extend from the house to the water's edge.

There is no salt spray here, but the garden is exposed to strong winds. The tough plants we chose take the wind in stride. The grasses achieve peak beauty in summer because they are exposed to full sun. But autumn here is beautiful, especially when the sun filters through leaves in stained-glass hues of mauve, gold, and copper. The Meyers even enjoy the garden on cold winter weekends when "the brown stalks of grasses creep out of the snow."

PREVIOUS SPREAD: *A zigzag boardwalk over the sand divides the designed garden near the house from the indigenous dune grass coming up from the beach.*

ABOVE: *Lake Michigan is seen over* Achillea filipendulina *'Coronation Gold',* Perovskia atriplicifolia, *and dune grass.*

OPPOSITE: *Autumn is resplendent with brilliant leaf color and dried seed heads of* Oxydendrum arboreum *(sourwood), yellow flowers of* Potentilla fruticosa *(golden cinquefoil), and the dried seed heads of* Solidago x *'Strahlenkrone' (goldenrod).*

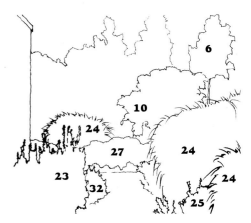

PREVIOUS SPREAD: *The blurred edges between softly textured masses of Panicum virgatum and Miscanthus sinensis purpurascens transform this ground plane into a multidimensional work of art, including the fourth dimension of time.*
VOLKMAR WENTZEL PHOTOGRAPH

PLANT KEY

TREES AND SHRUBS

1 PINUS SYLVESTRIS
   Scotch Pine

2 TAXUS X MEDIA 'DENSIFORMIS'
   Spreading Yew

3 POTENTILLA FRUTICOSA
   Bush Cinquefoil

4 PINUS THUNBERGIANA
   Japanese Black Pine

5 ILEX VERTICILLATA
   Winterberry Holly

6 GLEDITSIA TRIACANTHOS INERMIS
   'SHADEMASTER'
   Honeylocust

7 CORNUS SERICEA
   Red Osier Dogwood

8 JUNIPERUS CHINENSIS 'PFITZERIANA'
   Chinese Pfitzer Juniper

9 PINUS MUGO
   Swiss Mountain Pine

10 CERCIS CANADENSIS
   Eastern Redbud

11 MAHONIA AQUIFOLIUM 'KING'S
   RANSOM'
   Dwarf Oregon Grape Holly

12 AMELANCHIER CANADENSIS
   Shadblow Serviceberry

13 SALIX ELAEAGNOS
   Rosemary Willow, or Hoary Willow

14 COTONEASTER SALICIFOLIUS
   'SCARLET LEADER'
   Cotoneaster

PERENNIALS AND ORNAMENTAL GRASSES

15 AMMOPHILA BREVILIGULATA
   American Beach Grass

16 PEROVSKIA ATRIPLICIFOLIA
   Russian Sage

17 NEPETA X FAASSENII
   Catnip

18 BOLTONIA ASTEROIDES 'SNOWBANK'
   White Boltonia

19 ACHILLEA FILIPENDULINA
   'CORONATION GOLD'
   Yarrow

20 PANICUM VIRGATUM 'HAENSE
   HERMS'
   Red Switch Grass

21 PENNISETUM ALOPECUROIDES
   Fountain Grass

22 SESLERIA AUTUMNALIS
   Autumn Moor Grass

23 LYTHRUM SALICARIA 'MORDEN'S
   PINK'
   Loosestrife

24 MISCANTHUS SINENSIS 'GRACILLIMUS'
   Silver Grass

25 ACHILLEA MILLEFOLIUM 'RED
   BEAUTY'
   Yarrow

26 SEDUM X 'AUTUMN JOY'
   Stonecrop

27 RUDBECKIA FULGIDA 'GOLDSTURM'
   Black-eyed Susan

28 CHRYSANTHEMUM PACIFICUM
   Gold and Silver Chrysanthemum

29 FARGESIA NITIDA
   Blue Clump Bamboo

30 GERANIUM MACRORRHIZUM
   'SPESSART'
   Pale Pink Bigroot Geranium

31 CAREX FLACCA
   Blue-green Sedge

32 LAVANDULA ANGUSTIFOLIA
   Lavender

MISCELLANEOUS

33 RESIDENCE

34 ENTRY DRIVE

35 TENNIS COURT

36 BOARDWALK

3

2

1

2

2

15

1

1

36

17

16

18

33

29

11 11 11

30

24

24

31

14

1

2

2

2

2

16

5

19

14

16

6

27

29

12

12

27

22

6

17

2

2

5

34

2

21

6

23

26

27

13

22

15

20

22

7

9

9

28

20

25

9

4

10

28

9

20

24

4

1

20

13

22

8

1

1

20

24

1

19

35

1

9

1

24

14

8

1

28

24

18

20

↑

NORTH

0 4 8 12 16 feet

A pair of gardens at the National Arboretum's visitor center in Washington, D.C., the New American Garden on the east front and the Friendship Garden on the west front, set the tone for a visit to the arboretum and demonstrate important design principles that visitors can absorb and then apply to their own gardens. Because of the building's relatively small scale and residential look, we treated the gardens as residential prototypes.

The importance of scale is one of these gardens' significant lessons. They show how plants affect our perceptions of garden size and building

New American and Friendship Gardens

mass. For example, by placing taller plant masses toward the street we screened the front garden from traffic and reclaimed it for the use and enjoyment of those who work (or live) there. Also, by reducing the vertical scale of plants around the house we created the illusion that the house is more firmly anchored to the ground plane.

Defining garden spaces is another lesson. Since perennial plantings are dominant features in both gardens, we composed them in large enough masses to define garden spaces and to make the spaces more pleasant and useful. Our palette included *Helianthus angustifolius* (swamp sunflower), *Epimedium* spp. (barrenwort), *Aralia racemosa, Astilbe* spp. (false spirea), *Echinacea purpurea, Sesleria autumnalis* (autumn moor grass), and

Hakonechloa macra. Of course, the broad displays of single species also increase the gardens' drama. We planted single specimens and smaller plant clusters here and there for sculptural interest or as focal points.

Finally, these gardens provide perfect examples of how to achieve year-round interest. We selected and arranged plants that would change and surprise as the seasons unfold. We planted evergreens sparingly for contrast to the dramatic effects of winter's dried bouquets. We used lawn as a foil for planting areas and as an extension of the terrace for visitors who want to walk through the gardens.

PLANT KEY

TREES AND SHRUBS

1   NANDINA DOMESTICA
    Heavenly Bamboo
2   DEUTZIA GRACILIS 'NIKKO'
    Slender Deutzia
3   NANDINA DOMESTICA 'NANA PURPUREA'
    Dwarf Heavenly Bamboo
4   MAHONIA BEALII
    Leatherleaf Mahonia
5   ILEX X ATTENUATA 'FOSTERI'
    Foster Holly

PERENNIALS AND ORNAMENTAL GRASSES

6   BERGENIA CORDIFOLIA
    Heartleaf Bergenia
7   CAREX GLAUCA
    Sedge
8   MISCANTHUS SINENSIS 'VARIEGATUS'
    Silver Grass
9   CARYOPTERIS X CLANDONENSIS
    Bluebeard
10 LIRIOPE MUSCARI 'BIG BLUE'
    Big Blue Lily-Turf
11 IMPERATA CYLINDRICA 'RED BARON'
    Japanese Blood Grass
12 ECHINACEA PURPUREA
    Purple Coneflower
13 CHRYSOGONUM VIRGIANUM
    Golden Star

14 HOSTA SPP.
    Plantain Lily
15 ASTILBE SPP.
    False Spirea
16 SEDUM X 'AUTUMN JOY'
    Stonecrop
17 HOSTA X 'HONEYBELLS'
    Lavender Plantain Lily
18 SESLERIA AUTUMNALIS
    Autumn Moor Grass
19 MISCANTHUS SINENSIS 'MORNING LIGHT'
    Silver Grass
20 CRAMBE CORDIFOLIA
    Colewort
21 EUPATORIUM PURPUREUM
    Joe-Pye Weed
22 SALVIA NEMOROSA
    Sage
23 CALAMAGROSTIS ACUTIFLORA STRICTA
    Feather Reed Grass
24 PANICUM VIRGATUM 'HAENSE HERMS'
    Red Switch Grass
25 COREOPSIS VERTICILLATA 'MOONBEAM'
    Cutleaf Tickseed
26 LIATRIS SPICATA
    Gayfeather
27 PEROVSKIA ATRIPLICIFOLIA
    Russian Sage

28 RUDBECKIA FULGIDA 'GOLDSTURM'
    Black-eyed Susan
29 SPODIOPOGON SIBIRICUS
    Silver Spike Grass
30 MISCANTHUS SINENSIS PURPURASCENS
    Red Maiden Grass
31 EPIMEDIUM VERSICOLOR 'SULPHUREUM'
    Barrenwort
32 YUCCA FILAMENTOSA
    Adam's Needle
33 LAMIASTRUM GALEOBDOLON
    Yellow Archangel
34 TIARELLA CORDIFOLIA
    Foam Flower
35 CAREX MORROWII 'VARIEGATA'
    Japanese Sedge

ANNUALS

36 LANTANA MONTEVIDENSIS
    Trailing Lantana/Shrub Verbena

MISCELLANEOUS

37 VISITOR'S CENTER
38 SCULPTURE
39 BENCH

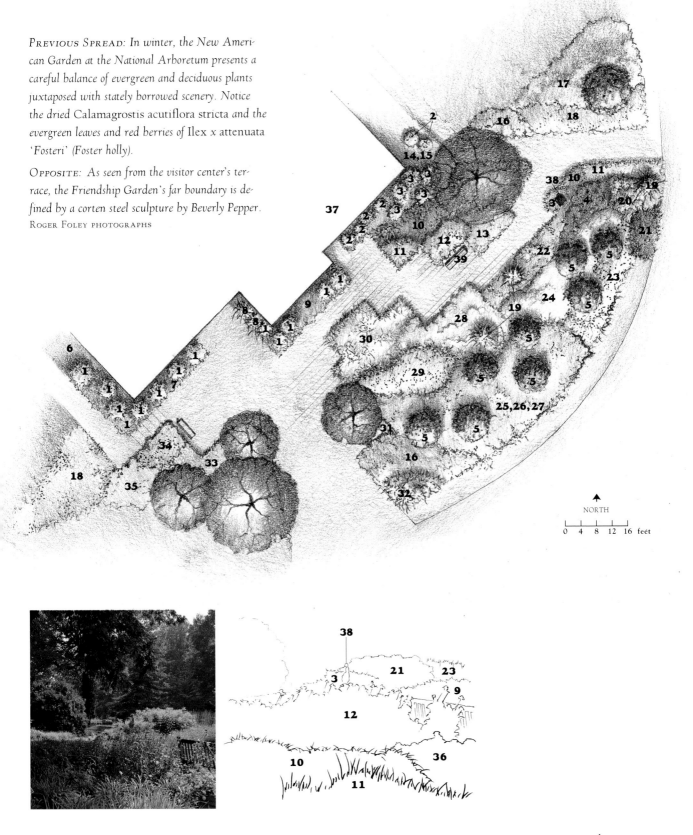

PREVIOUS SPREAD: *In winter, the New American Garden at the National Arboretum presents a careful balance of evergreen and deciduous plants juxtaposed with stately borrowed scenery. Notice the dried Calamagrostis acutiflora stricta and the evergreen leaves and red berries of Ilex x attenuata 'Fosteri' (Foster holly).*

OPPOSITE: *As seen from the visitor center's terrace, the Friendship Garden's far boundary is defined by a corten steel sculpture by Beverly Pepper.*
ROGER FOLEY PHOTOGRAPHS

NORTH

0 4 8 12 16 feet

THE OEHME GARDEN

Wolfgang's half-acre property in Towson, Maryland, a suburb of Baltimore, is more than a garden; it is a monument to his boundless passion for plants. In addition to displays of favorite plants, Wolfgang has created a plant nursery, a horticultural laboratory, a vegetable garden, and an open-air classroom, where he eagerly shares his passion with visitors from around the world. His garden is even a mini–wildlife haven—a place where friends and clients come when they need snails, frogs, tadpoles, and other ecology-balancing creatures for their own gardens.

When Wolfgang bought the house in 1988, the "landscaping" consisted only of lawn (which he quickly removed) and one large pine tree in front. He sculpted the sloping area behind the house to create terraces, connected the terraces with steps, and started a planting frenzy that continues to this day with at least 250 plant varieties. The garden is a continuous work in progress—a dynamic place filled with unusual plants and horticultural surprises.

Visitors first see the back garden from an elevated deck behind the house. This overview is striking because of Wolfgang's masterful placement of plants in large, free-form groupings: *Ligularia dentata* 'Desdemona', *Spodiopogon sibiricus*, *Lysimachia clethroides* (gooseneck loosestrife), *Silphium perfoliatum* (dock rosinweed), *Pennisetum alopecuroides* 'Moudry', *Aralia cordata* (Japanese spikenard), *Evodia hupehensis* (bee-bee tree), *Trachystemon orientale* (eastern borage), and many others. After the visitor steps down from the deck to inspect the plants up close, surprises await at every turn, including the evergreen *Senecio aureus*, which has yellow blossoms in spring and provides great groundcover for moist

places, and the unusual *Polygonum polymorphum* (fleece flower)—not yet listed in any literature—that blooms white all summer. Other seasonal surprises include the bold yarrowlike leaves and white flowers of *Tanacetum macrophyllum* and the red fruit of *Euonymus planipes* (Sachalin euonymus). The blossoms of the harlequin glory-bower tree, *Clerodendron trichotomum*, is a magnet for butterflies during August and September. Large clumps of *Fargesia nitida*, Wolfgang's signature plant, provide accents throughout the garden.

ABOVE AND OPPOSITE: ROGER FOLEY

*We started out with a basically beautiful landscape
and wound up with a great work of art.
I especially love the ornamental grasses—they are a
breath of fresh air in a vacuum of tradition
here on the East Coast.*

—KAREN OFFUTT

It is hard to imagine a more beautiful country setting than this quiet hillside bordered by pasture and woodland near Baltimore, Maryland. We decided to create a planting design that would frame distant views and enhance borrowed scenery.

THE MR. AND MRS. NELSON OFFUTT GARDEN

Wolfgang first visited the property in October 1987. He found what Mrs. Offutt describes as "an English perennial garden." Although Wolfgang made no comment after surveying the scene, she says he later "grassed" it in.

We drew our plan over the winter and built the swimming pool the following summer. One year later, we were ready to plant. We enlarged and regraded the lawn, opening up broad views of rolling pastures and woods that stretch to the horizon. We planted massive sweeps of perennials to exaggerate the slopes and blur the tran-

LEFT AND FOLLOWING SPREAD: *The all-season planting shown here is a metaphor for the American meadow. The "meadow" sweeps seamlessly into the pasture beyond and makes the pasture fence disappear.*
ROGER FOLEY PHOTOGRAPHS

sition from the terraces and lawn around the house to pasture and meadow. Mrs. Offutt describes the resulting planted areas as "huge." She says, in particular, that the masses of *Achillea filipendulina* give her great pleasure. She is also partial to *Caryopteris* x *clandonensis, Acanthus hungaricus, Calamagrostis brachytricha* (reed grass), and *Erianthus ravennae* (ravenna grass). Her favorite tree is the *Rhus chinensis* 'September Beauty' (Chinese sumac), which

CAROLINE SEGUI

she refers to as a miracle tree because of its dramatic year-round qualities: lustrous green foliage in spring and summer; large, cream-colored flowers in August and September; and radiant clusters of orange-to-red fruit throughout the winter.

We used a striking but dangerous plant in this garden: *Heracleum mantegazzianum* (giant hogweed). It blooms ten feet in the air, with white flowers that resemble a giant Queen Anne's lace. It is poisonous to the touch on hot summer days, so one must wear long pants and gloves when working near it. When lit at night, Mrs. Offutt says, "It is unbeatable." Wolfgang relishes gardening dangerously.

A simple white farm fence separates the pasture from the garden. In summer it disappears completely behind mounds of perennials. You would think the horses could gallop right through the leaves and flowers to the house.

ROGER FOLEY

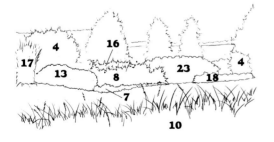

Mrs. Offutt doesn't miss her English borders. They were too much work, and they also deprived her of having something in bloom most of the year. She loves the soft blues, mauves, yellows, and faded pinks of the new garden. But she also likes high contrast: the pairing of hot-pink *Lagerstroemia indica* 'Sioux' (crape myrtle) and *Rudbeckia fulgida* 'Goldsturm' is especially striking.

Planting a garden in the foreground of such an important view requires the strength of simplicity. The huge meadowlike drifts of color in this garden match the scale of the rest of the landscape and draw the garden into harmony with its "borrowed scenery." For me, the result is a complete garden world.

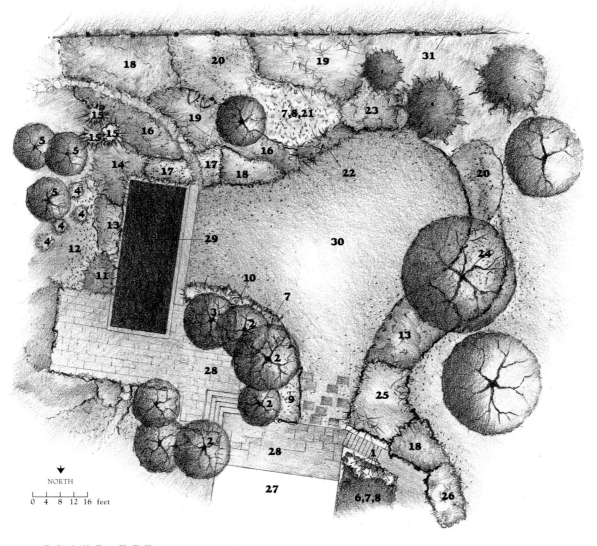

NORTH

0 4 8 12 16 feet

PLANT KEY

TREES AND SHRUBS

1 NANDINA DOMESTICA
   Heavenly Bamboo

2 AMELANCHIER CANADENSIS
   Shadblow Serviceberry

3 CORNUS KOUSA
   Kousa Dogwood

4 VIBURNUM DILATATUM
   Linden Viburnum

5 ARALIA SPINOSA
   Devil's Walking Stick

PERENNIALS AND ORNAMENTAL
GRASSES

6 CERATOSTIGMA PLUMBAGINOIDES
   Leadwort

7 COREOPSIS VERTICILLATA
   'MOONBEAM'
   Cutleaf Tickseed

8 PEROVSKIA ATRIPLICIFOLIA
   Russian Sage

9 STOKESIA LAEVIS 'BLUE DANUBE'
   Blue Stokes' Aster

10 PENNISETUM ALOPECUROIDES
    Fountain Grass

11 YUCCA FILAMENTOSA
    Adam's Needle

12 RUDBECKIA FULGIDA 'GOLDSTURM'
    Black-eyed Susan

13 SEDUM X 'AUTUMN JOY'
    Stonecrop

14 PENNISETUM ORIENTALE
    Fountain Grass

15 MISCANTHUS SINENSIS 'GRACILLIMUS'
    Japanese Maiden Grass

16 LYTHRUM SALICARIA 'MORDEN'S
    PINK'
    Loosestrife

17 CALAMAGROSTIS X ACUTIFLORA
    'KARL FOERSTER'
    Feather Reed Grass

18 ACHILLEA FILIPENDULINA
    'CORONATION GOLD'
    Coronation Gold Yarrow

19 HEMEROCALLIS SPP.
    Daylily

20 PANICUM VIRGATUM
    Switch Grass

21 LIATRIS SPICATA
    Gayfeather

22 MISCANTHUS SINENSIS 'YAKU JIMA'
    Silver Grass

23 EUPATORIUM PURPUREUM
    Joe-Pye Weed

24 ASTILBE ARENDSII 'DIAMANT'
    White False Spiraea

25 MISCANTHUS SINENSIS PURPURASCENS
    Red Maiden Grass

26 PENNISETUM ALOPECUROIDES
    VIRIDESCENS
    *Black-seeded Fountain
    Grass*

MISCELLANEOUS

27 RESIDENCE

28 TERRACE

29 SWIMMING POOL

30 LAWN

31 FENCE

PARADISE MANOR APARTMENTS

*It's a demonstration of what good architects, and landscape architects, can do when
given a chance, even with a limited budget and even in the most restricted circumstances.
In the world of Paradise Manor this counts as a major, humanizing transformation:
Where before there was almost nothing, there is now a handsome sequence of useful
spaces clearly dedicated to the public realm.*

—BENJAMIN FORGEY, *THE WASHINGTON POST,* JULY 4, 1992

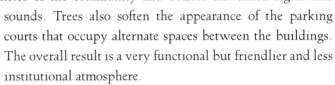

Paradise Manor's transformation proves dramatically that planting not only enhances a community's physical appearance but also contributes to its social well-being. This Washington, D.C., community of fifteen buildings and more than six hundred garden apartments had fallen into an extreme state of physical blight and social deterioration when we, along with a team of developers, architects, and other specialists, were invited to participate in a rescue effort (see photograph below). The team's goal, now achieved, was to reestablish a safe, supportive, and attractive living environment.

We designed a grand pedestrian promenade that knits the entire community together and provides access to seven landscaped courtyards—one between each pair of buildings. The plants we selected complement the redesigned building facades and new site amenities. We chose distinctive palettes of perennials and ornamental grasses to give each courtyard a sense of individuality. The parklike planting, combined with comfortable benches, ornamental fencing, and traditional outdoor light fixtures, attracts residents to the courtyards for informal neighborhood activities. Trees offer shade and soften the scale of the dense development. We also provided ample swaths of lawn for the residents' play and passive recreation.

The plantings spill out of the courtyards into common areas along the promenade. Street trees define the perimeter of the community and deflect unwanted sights and

sounds. Trees also soften the appearance of the parking courts that occupy alternate spaces between the buildings. The overall result is a very functional but friendlier and less institutional atmosphere.

*We thought the overall theme of the garden should suggest,
but not imitate, the history of the place—
an eastern Long Island shore and farmland community.
We envisioned a sensuous but rustic garden with the feeling
of farmland gone to meadowland. In other words,
a little like a neglected farm.*

—CAROLE RIFKIND

THE RICHARD AND CAROLE RIFKIND GARDEN

The Rifkinds came to us with a sophisticated vision of what the planting plan for their garden should achieve and a tentative list of plants to support it.

Their rustic vision for the garden complemented its sensitive environment—just a thousand feet from the ocean between plant-covered dunes. They came upon the idea of re-creating a neglected-farmhouse look while visiting a charming old apple orchard near their house. They decided to keep many of the existing plants around the house, including an old apple tree, several crabapple trees, a grouping of *Pinus thunbergiana* (Japanese black pine), *Kalmia latifolia* (mountain laurel), a collection of *Rhododendron* spp. (rhododendrons), *Lonicera* spp. (honeysuckle), *Elaeagnus angustifolia* (Russian olive), and *Sassafras* sp. (sassafras). Following the overall farmland theme, their idea for privacy screening along property boundaries was to create an informal hedgerow to be made up of *Myrica pensylvanica* (northern bayberry), *Rosa rugosa* (rugosa rose), and *Juniperus virginiana* (eastern red cedar).

The Rifkinds' initial plant list further defined the qualities of the garden they had in mind. They listed plants that are durable, easy to maintain, and adapt-

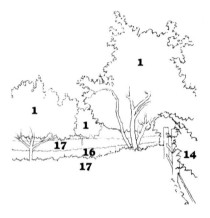

able to the local climate and soils. They did not plan a vegetable garden, but what they described for part of the backyard was clearly a metaphor for one. The list did include edibles such as corn, asparagus, grapes, raspberries, and rhubarb.

After hearing the Rifkinds describe their visit to the old apple orchard, we decided to create a stylized orchard across the middle of the backyard by keeping the apple and crabapple trees and adding new trees: two *Malus* 'Granny Smith', two *Malus* 'Primo', one *Malus* 'Baldwin', and one *Malus* 'Gravenstein'. The new orchard reinforces the farm image and cleverly screens the swimming pool from the rest of the garden. We seeded the ground under the trees with wildflowers to enhance the farm look. Today, maintenance is limited to rough mowing of the lawn.

Wolfgang used plants that look like vegetables when he chose plants for the rest of the garden: *Arundo donax variegata* (striped giant reed), *Inula magnifica* 'Sonnenspeer' (elecampagne), *Origanum laevigatum* 'Herrenhausen' (marjoram), *Miscanthus sinensis,* and *Tanacetum macrophyllum.* Plants he chose to promote the "meadow" look include *Boltonia asteroides* 'Snowbank', *Alcea rosea* (hollyhock), *Eupatorium fistulosum* 'Gateway' (joe-pye weed), *Campanula punctata* (bellflower), and *Liatris pycnostachya* (gayfeather).

We responded to the Rifkinds' request for soft edges by adding *Elaeagnus umbellatus* (autumn olive), *Hydrangea paniculata* 'Tardiva' (panicle hydrangea), *Viburnum* x *pragense,* *Chionanthus retusus* (Chinese fringe tree), and *Juniperus virginiana* (eastern red cedar).

Today, the Rifkinds' very particular vision is a reality—a rustic "meadow," far from the frantic pace of their weekdays in busy Manhattan.

PREVIOUS SPREAD: *Petals from an old ornamental cherry tree rain down on the front terrace, the rustic furniture, and the path to the front door in early spring.*

RIGHT: *Planting that resembles a meadow is created with* Arundo donax variegata *(striped giant reed),* Artemisia *'Powis Castle', and* Hibiscus moscheutos *(rose mallow).*

PREVIOUS SPREAD, ABOVE, AND RIGHT: RICHARD FELBER PHOTOGRAPHS

PLANT KEY

TREES AND SHRUBS

1 MALUS SPP.
   Apple Tree

2 CORNUS MAS
   Cornelian Cherry

PERENNIALS AND ORNAMENTAL GRASSES

3 LIRIOPE MUSCARI 'BIG BLUE'
   Lily-Turf

4 FARGESIA NITIDA
   Blue Clump Bamboo

5 TOVARA VIRGINIANA
   Polygonum Painter's Palette

6 PENNISETUM ALOPECUROIDES
   Fountain Grass

7 MISCANTHUS SINENSIS GIGANTEUS
   Giant Chinese Silver Grass

8 HELICTOTRICHON SEMPERVIRENS
   Blue Oat Grass

9 LAVANDULA ANGUSTIFOLIA 'HIDCOTE'
   Lavender

10 LIATRIS SPICATA
    Gayfeather

11 NEPETA X FAASSENII
    Catnip

12 PEROVSKIA ATRIPLICIFOLIA
    Russian Sage

13 BRUNNERA MACROPHYLLA
    Siberian Bugloss

VINES

14 CLEMATIS SPP.
    Clematis

MISCELLANEOUS

15 RESIDENCE

16 LAWN

17 ROUGH LAWN

18 FENCE

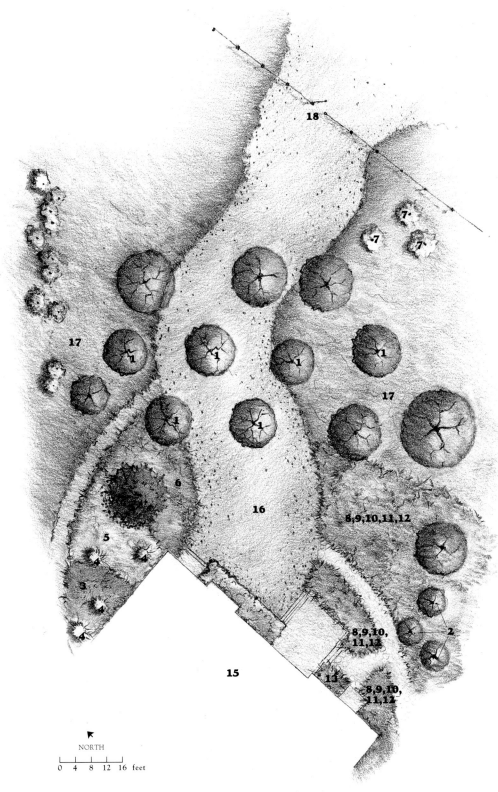

NORTH

0 4 8 12 16 feet

In 1985, I spoke to members of the New York Botanical Garden about our concept of the New American Garden. It happened that Amanda Burden, then a vice president of the Battery Park City Authority, was in the audience. Soon after the lecture she called, graciously endorsing the planting philosophy I had described, and expressed a special interest in one of the gardens I had shown, Alex and Carole Rosenberg's garden on Long Island's Mecox Bay (see photograph, page 168). She saw an appealing similarity between the Rosenbergs' waterfront garden

NELSON A. ROCKEFELLER PARK

and the yet-to-be-designed Nelson A. Rockefeller Park on the Hudson River at Battery Park City. The seaside feeling we achieved for the Rosenbergs matched her image of what the new park should be—a subtle reminder of the beach environment that flourished on the site centuries ago. Before we knew it, Amanda Burden invited us to design the landscaping for the park. The plants we chose for the areas along the esplanade reinforce the seaside spirit she hoped to evoke. They include *Panicum virgatum*, *Pinus thunbergiana* (Japanese black pine), *Calamagrostis acutiflora stricta*, and *Carex muskingumensis* (palm sedge).

Whereas the riverside esplanade is reminiscent of the seashore, the "upland" reaches of the park feature plants that are native to

another local environment, the Hudson River Valley. Our plant selections for those areas include *Amelanchier canadensis* (shadblow serviceberry), *Betula nigra* (river birch), *Ginkgo biloba* (maidenhair tree), *Crataegus phaenopyrum* (Washington hawthorn), and *Symphoricarpos albus* (common snowberry).

The park's appearance today belies the fact that it sits atop a landfill in the Hudson River. When we first saw the site it was a flat and dusty expanse of sand. Our first design challenge was to shape the land for a softer, more natural, appearance. We devised a subtle pattern of berms and gentle slopes that show the plants to better advantage and give them more height. Gently rolling dunelike forms along the riverside esplanade enhance the shoreline image.

The respect given this park by users is evidence of its success. Although it attracts multitudes year-round for sports, entertainment, and passive recreation, it retains the natural image we originally envisioned: a timeless seashore behind rolling meadows, lush swaths of flowering perennials, and welcoming carpets of lawn.

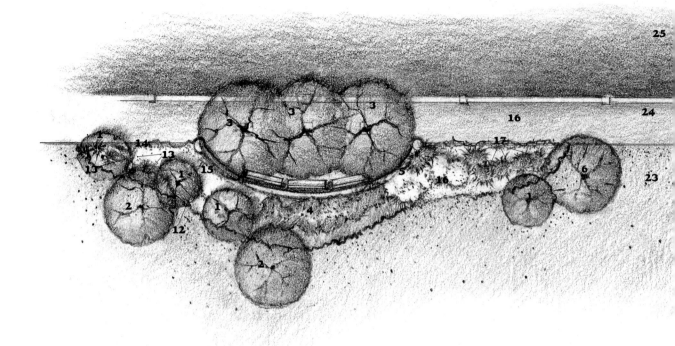

PLANT KEY

TREES AND SHRUBS

1 CRATAEGUS PHAENOPYRUM
   Washington Hawthorn

2 GINKGO BILOBA
   Maidenhair Tree

3 SOPHORA JAPONICA
   Japanese Pagoda Tree

4 ROSA 'BONICA'
   Meidiland Bonica Rose

5 BUDDLEIA DAVIDII 'EMPIRE BLUE'
   Butterfly Bush

6 NYSSA SYLVATICA
   Black Gum

7 MALUS 'DONALD WYMAN'
   Donald Wyman Crab Apple

8 PINUS THUNBERGIANA
   Japanese Black Pine

9 HIPPOPHAE RHAMNOIDES
   Sea Buckthorn

10 CEDRUS LIBANI
   Cedar of Lebanon

11 CYTISUS X PRAECOX
   Warminster Broom

PERENNIALS AND ORNAMENTAL GRASSES

12 ARCTOSTAPHYLOS UVA-URSI
   Bearberry

13 SPODIOPOGON SIBIRICUS
   Silver Spike Grass

14 PEROVSKIA ATRIPLICIFOLIA
   Russian Sage,
   interplanted with
   COREOPSIS VERTICILLATA 'MOONBEAM'
   Cutleaf Tickseed

15 SYMPHORICARPOS X CHENAULTI 'HANCOCK'
   Chenault Coralberry

16 MOLINIA CAERULEA ARUNDINACEA 'WINDSPIEL'
   Tall Purple Moor Grass

17 MISCANTHUS SINENSIS GIGANTEUS
   Giant Chinese Silver Grass

18 CAREX MUSKINGUMENSIS
   Palm Sedge

19 CAREX PENDULA
   Drooping Sedge

20 CAREX MORROWII VARIEGATA
   Variegated Japanese Sedge

21 MISCANTHUS SINENSIS 'GRAZIELLA'
   Silver Grass

22 LYTHRUM SALICARIA 'MORDEN'S PINK'
   Loosestrife

MISCELLANEOUS

23 LAWN

24 ESPLANADE

25 HUDSON RIVER

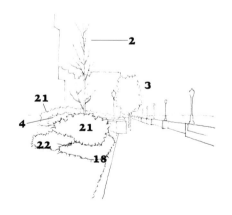

THE CAROLE AND ALEX ROSENBERG TERRACE

The beautiful plantings on our penthouse terrace have enhanced our view and our moments of thought and relaxation. Being able to look out at a picture-postcard garden view the year round, with the skyline of Manhattan as a backdrop, is something we cherish.

—CAROLE ROSENBERG

When Wolfgang and I first saw this terrace it was a long, narrow, unadorned space overlooking the city. It was exposed to the elements and open to direct view from nearby buildings. Its only improvement was a red quarry tile floor, which we agreed was a good base for a container garden. Our objectives were to emphasize the panoramic views of the Manhattan skyline and Central Park, screen out unwanted views and viewers, and break up the corridor-like appearance of the space. The design tools we selected include arbors, lattice side screens, container plants, and sculpture.

We designed the arbors and placed them in an intermittent pattern, which creates an illusion of outdoor rooms. The arbors slope from the blank building wall to the outside terrace edge. The resulting irregular volume of sheltered spaces adds a welcome sense of protection when viewed from the solarium at one end of the garden (the only point of access). The lattice side screens further define the arbor "rooms" and screen out unwanted views. *Wisteria floribunda* (Japanese wisteria), *Clematis* cultivars, and *Polygonum aubertii* cover the arbors and cast shadowy patterns on the tile floor.

The container plants we selected include: *Pennisetum alopecuroides* 'Moudry', *Panicum virgatum* 'Haense Herms', *Crataegus phaenopyrum* (Washington hawthorne), and *Coreopsis verticillata* 'Moonbeam'. As in our earth-bound gardens, we layered masses of plants to accentuate the scale. The composition begins in the solarium with a collection of indoor plants on a beautiful antique French plant stand. The larger containers and taller trees occupy the middle part of the garden under the arbors. A perennial border defines an open dining area at the far end of the garden, where guests enjoy dramatic views of midtown Manhattan and Central Park.

Sculptures from the Rosenbergs' extensive collection adorn the terrace and provide wonderful contrasts in scale. Mid-terrace, a bronze torso by Henry Moore provides a glorious focal point and poses handsomely among plantings of *Pinus thunbergiana* (Japanese black pine), *Lamium galeobdolon* (yellow archangel), and *Panicum virgatum* 'Haense Herms'.

*I don't yearn for English borders; coming from
Australia, I want a different feeling. Melbourne
with its temperate climate labors under the
English influence. I wanted to go to a big,
swooping American gesture.
I adore the garden and actually spend a lot of time
taking in its differences. From week to week in
spring and summer, and even in winter, the
changes are terrifyingly quick, and I'm filled with
this feeling of 'seize the day'!*

—ROSITA TRINCA

THE SIMON AND ROSITA TRINCA GARDEN

When Wolfgang and I first saw this two-acre site on a corner lot in Connecticut, a driveway bisected the front yard like a highway. It entered the property through piers at one corner of the property, passed the front door midway along its run, and ended on the opposite corner. It is no wonder the Trincas felt they were living in the midst of a network of roads.

The front yard was framed on two sides by mature *Fagus grandiflora* (American beech), and the driveway was lined with shocking pink kurume azaleas. Drainage was poor and the soil needed amending.

We removed two-thirds of the driveway and relocated the turnaround near the garage where we consolidated it with guest and service parking. This liberated the land in front of the house for masses of plantings, through which we designed a broad walk to the front door. Because the Trincas agreed to eliminate the entire front lawn, we were able to transform an ordinary yard with tall shrubs planted tightly against the house into a grand, relaxed garden with small flowering trees, ornamental grasses, and perennials that radiate from the house to the street. The planting is especially beautiful when viewed from the house against the dark backdrop of *Fagus grandiflora* and *Fagus sylvatica* 'Cuprea' (copper beech) that line the street.

The backyard slopes from the house to a line of *Pinus strobus* (eastern white pine) along the property line. A swimming pool occupies the far left-hand corner of the property and a tennis court lies to the right. Beyond the pool, a dramatic "borrowed view" of a golf course stretches as far as the eye can see. The backdrop of trees behind the tennis court is an extension of the screen that protects the front yard from the street.

On either side of the backyard we replaced lawn with broad planting areas. We linked the remaining small area of lawn to the main terrace with grass steps. Large stone planters flank the steps and act as decorative "cheek" walls. To hide the swimming pool, frame the distant view of the golf course, and further buffer the garden from the sights and sounds of the street, we used foreground planting of *Betula nigra, Viburnum* x *pragense, Viburnum prunifolium* (black haw viburnum), *Chelone lyonii* (turtle head), and *Vernonia noveboracensis* (New York ironweed). This daring approach to planting design resulted in the "big, swooping American gesture" that Mrs. Trinca envisioned when we first talked about the garden.

The Trincas wanted their garden to make a revolutionary statement. Mrs. Trinca calls the result a "radical plan," and credits the perennial plantings with giving her garden an "other-worldly" quality. The Trincas' favorite perennials are summer-blooming *Nepeta sibirica* and *Perovskia atriplicifolia*. In the heat of summer they bloom in what Mrs. Trinca describes as a "lovely blue haze."

The Trincas' garden is a truly American landscape that perfectly complements the relaxed charm of their classic Arts and Crafts residence.

PREVIOUS SPREAD: Buddleia davidii *(butterfly bush),* Rudbeckia fulgida, *and an old weeping willow glow like stained glass in the early morning light, framing the borrowed view of a golf course in the distance.*

RIGHT: Helianthus spp. *(sunflower)* and Pennisetum alopecuroides 'Moudry' *edge this stepping-stone path through the garden.*

OPPOSITE: *Pea gravel steps, edged with cobbles and banked with* Lysimachia clethroides *(gooseneck loosestrife),* Buddleia davidii *(butterfly bush), and* Rudbeckia fulgida *lead to the great lawn at the back garden.*
RICHARD FELBER PHOTOGRAPHS

PLANT KEY

TREES AND SHRUBS

1 TAXUS BACCATA 'REPANDENS'
Spreading English Yew

2 MAHONIA AQUIFOLIUM
Oregon Grape Holly

3 NANDINA DOMESTICA
Heavenly Bamboo

4 COTONEASTER SALICIFOLIUS 'SCARLET LEADER'
Cotoneaster

5 FRANKLINIA ALATAMAHA
Franklin Tree

6 BUDDLEIA DAVIDII
Butterfly Bush

7 SYRINGA RETICULATA
Japanese Tree Lilac

8 JASMINUM NUDIFLORUM
Jasmine

9 STEWARTIA PSEUDOCAMELLIA
Japanese Stewartia

10 VIBURNUM SETIGERUM
Tea Viburnum

11 CHIMONANTHUS PRAECOX
Wintersweet

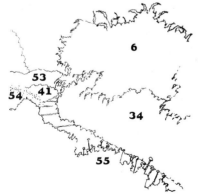

12 BETULA NIGRA 'HERITAGE'
River Birch

13 CORNUS SERICEA
Red-Osier Dogwood

14 CORNUS KOUSA
Kousa Dogwood

15 HYDRANGEA ARBORESCENS 'ANNABELLE'
Smooth Hydrangea

PERENNIALS AND ORNAMENTAL GRASSES

16 CAREX MORROWII
Japanese Sedge

17 EPIMEDIUM SPP.
Barrenwort

18 FARGESIA NITIDA
Blue Clump Bamboo

19 PENNISETUM ALOPECUROIDES
Fountain Grass

20 EUPHORBIA PALUSTRIS
Spurge

21 CALAMAGROSTIS ACUTIFLORA STRICTA
Feather Reed Grass

22 YUCCA FILAMENTOSA
Adam's Needle

23 ARTEMISIA ARBORESCENS 'POWIS CASTLE'
Wormwood

24 AJUGA REPTANS
Bugle Weed

25 CERATOSTIGMA PLUMBAGINOIDES
Leadwort

26 BRUNNERA MACROPHYLLA
Siberian Bugloss

27 MISCANTHUS SINENSIS
Silver Grass

28 HELLEBORUS ORIENTALIS
Lenten Rose

29 HOSTA PLANTAGINEA
Plantain Lily

30 NEPETA X FAASSENII
Catnip

31 ERYNGIUM ALPINUM 'AMETHYST'
Sea Holly

32 CASSIA MARILANDICA
Wild Senna

33 GERANIUM MACRORRHIZUM 'SPESSART'
Pale Pink Bigroot Geranium

34 CARYOPTERIS X CLANDONENSIS 'LONGWOOD BLUE'
Bluebeard

35 LAVANDULA ANGUSTIFOLIA 'HIDCOTE'
Lavender

36 ASTER ERICOIDES
Heath Aster

37 ALLIUM TUBEROSUM
Ornamental Onion

38 CALAMINTHA NEPETOIDES 'GOTTLIEB FRIEDKUND'
Dwarf Flowering Mint

39 SEDUM X 'AUTUMN JOY'
Stonecrop

40 HELIANTHUS ANGUSTIFOLIUS
Swamp Sunflower

41 LYSIMACHIA CLETHROIDES
Gooseneck Loosestrife

42 EUPATORIUM FISTULOSUM 'GATEWAY'
Joe-Pye Weed

43 IRIS PSEUDACORUS
Yellow Flag Iris

44 POLYGONATUM BIFLORUM
Solomon's Seal

45 PRIMULA X BULLESIANA
Primrose

46 MIXED PERENNIAL BORDER

47 CHELONE LYONII
Turtle-Head

48 LOBELIA CARDINALIS
Cardinal Flower

49 MACLEAYA CORDATA
Plume Poppy

50 CAREX PENDULA
Drooping Sedge

51 ACANTHUS HUNGARICUS
Bear's-Breech

52 HIBISCUS MOSCHEUTOS
Rose Mallow

53 BOLTONIA ASTEROIDES 'SNOWBANK'
White Boltonia

54 PANICUM VIRGATUM 'HAENSE HERMS'
Red Switch Grass

55 RUDBECKIA FULGIDA 'GOLDSTURM'
Black-eyed Susan

MISCELLANEOUS

56 RESIDENCE

57 DRIVEWAY

58 LILY POOL

59 STONE TERRACE

60 LAWN STEPS

61 LAWN

62 SWIMMING POOL

PREVIOUS SPREAD: Boltonia asteroides 'Snowbank', Artemesia 'Powis Castle', and Caryopteris x clandonensis flank the gravel steps while 'New Dawn' roses and white clematis cascade over the arbor on the right to create this romantic summer scene. PREVIOUS SPREAD AND LEFT: RICHARD FELBER PHOTOGRAPHS

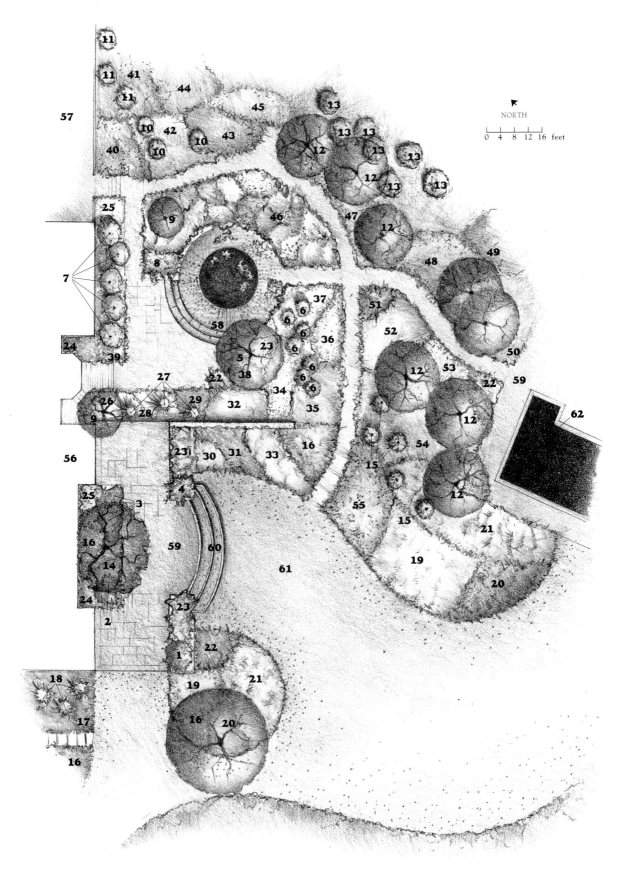

NORTH

0 4 8 12 16 feet

Creative clients always stimulate us to greater innovation in our use of plants. The Ulfelders' garden is a creative success because Mr. and Mrs. Ulfelder became our design partners from the very beginning. Each of us came up with a list of our favorite plants, and after spirited review and discussions of alternatives, we drew a plan that satisfied everyone.

A road that is little more than a wide trail approaches this northern Virginia property through woods abutting the Potomac River.

THE SUSAN AND JOHN ULFELDER GARDEN

The driveway descends steeply to a circular turnaround in front of the house. The house is built into the slope that is now a hillside garden. No property boundaries or fences are visible, and woods obscure the view of neighboring houses.

Before my first meeting with the Ulfelders the entire cleared area around the house, including a septic field and all bare slopes, had been hydro-seeded for erosion control. Some sod had been placed near the house, and a few *Rhododendron* spp. (azaleas) were planted at the building foundation to satisfy occupancy permit requirements. Otherwise, we started designing with a clean slate.

Because there is no public sewerage in the area a septic system was required. The septic field is located at the top of the hill to the right as one enters the property. This presented a unique landscaping challenge. Because regulations prohibit trees or shrubs on a septic field, we turned it into a natural garden—a true metaphor for the American meadow. A perennial garden is perfectly adaptable to such a flat, open area. Again, we found the natural approach to be better.

The Ulfelders did not want any lawn. With the possible exception of the flat septic field, lawn made no sense at all on such a steep site. The all-season garden we planted cascades with *Polygonum affine* (Himalayan fleece flower), *Miscanthus sinensis* 'Roland', *Lamium galeobdolon* (yellow archangel), *Achillea filipendulina* 'Moonshine', and *Aster frikartii* 'Mönch' (hardy purple aster). The trees and shrubs we planted include *Franklinia alatamaha* (franklin tree), *Ilex* x 'Nellie R. Stevens' (Nellie R. Stevens holly), *Hamamelis* x *intermedia* 'Arnold Promise' (witch hazel), *Lagerstroemia indica* 'Natchez' (crape myrtle), and *Hydrangea aspera* (hydrangea).

Mrs. Ulfelder exclaims, "The planting is exquisite!" Her favorites are *Cornus kousa* and the ornamental grasses that blow in the wind and produce seed for the birds. She says the *Buddleia davidii* 'Charming Summer' (butterfly bush) is always covered with Monarch butterflies and that bluebirds and hummingbirds dine on its berries and nectar. During a recent blizzard only the dried catkins of the grasses were visible above the snow, and birds were perched on them busily eating the seeds.

As in many gardens nowadays, deer have become a problem. We made some adjustments in the planting plan to discourage them and moved the hosta collection to a protected spot close to the house. Fortunately, the deer avoid the ornamental grasses and the much-prized *Fargesia nitida*.

The garden grew lush and covered all the mulch within two years. After the third year the Ulfelders felt it was fully mature. This challenging experiment in designing as a team is now a beautiful garden that begins on a hillside clearing, moves across steep slopes, and merges naturally with the surrounding woods.

The top of the wall that retains the septic field is softened with Cotoneaster salicifolius *'Scarlet Leader' (willowleaf cotoneaster), and* Aster frikartii *'Mönch' (hardy purple aster).*
PREVIOUS SPREAD AND OPPOSITE: ROGER FOLEY PHOTOGRAPHS

PLANT KEY

TREES AND SHRUBS

1. ILEX X 'NELLIE R. STEVENS'
   Nellie R. Stevens Holly

2. CORNUS KOUSA
   Kousa Dogwood

3. HAMAMELIS X INTERMEDIA 'ARNOLD PROMISE'
   Chinese Witch Hazel

4. NANDINA DOMESTICA 'COMPACTA NANA'
   Dwarf Heavenly Bamboo

5. LAGERSTROEMIA INDICA 'NATCHEZ'
   Natchez Crape Myrtle

6. MAHONIA BEALII
   Leatherleaf Mahonia

7. MAGNOLIA VIRGINIANA
   Sweet Bay Magnolia

8. COTONEASTER SALICIFOLIUS 'SCARLET LEADER'
   Willowleaf Cotoneaster

9. TSUGA CANADENSIS
   Canadian Hemlock

10. MAGNOLIA GRANDIFLORA 'BROWN BEAUTY'
    Southern Magnolia

PERENNIALS AND ORNAMENTAL GRASSES

11. YUCCA FILAMENTOSA
    Adam's Needle

12. SEDUM X 'AUTUMN JOY'
    Stonecrop

13. SPODIOPOGON SIBIRICUS
    Silver Spike Grass

14. CERATOSTIGMA PLUMBAGINOIDES
    Leadwort

15. LIRIOPE MUSCARI 'BIG BLUE'
    Lily-Turf

16. ASTER X FRIKARTII 'MÖNCH'
    Hardy Purple Aster

17. COREOPSIS VERTICILLATA 'MOONBEAM'
    Cutleaf Tickseed

18. ACHILLEA FILIPENDULINA 'MOONSHINE'
    Yarrow

19. LYTHRUM SALICARIA 'MORDEN'S ROSE'
    Rose Loosestrife

20. BOLTONIA ASTEROIDES 'SNOWBANK'
    White Boltonia

21. SESLERIA AUTUMNALIS
    Autumn Moor Grass

22. ACANTHUS HUNGARICUS
    Bear's-Breech

23. PANICUM VIRGATUM 'HAENSE HERMS'
    Red Switch Grass

24. SEDUM X 'RUBY GLOW'
    Stonecrop

25. CALAMAGROSTIS ACUTIFLORA STRICTA
    Feather Reed Grass

26. POLYGONUM AFFINE
    Himaleyan Fleece Flower

27. FARGESIA NITIDA
    Blue Clump Bamboo

28. MOLINIA CAERULEA ARUNDINACEA 'WINDSPIEL'
    Tall Purple Moor Grass

29. HOSTA VENTRICOSA
    Plantain Lily

30. ASTILBE CHINENSIS 'FINALE'
    False Spiraea

31. LAMIUM GALEOBDOLON
    Yellow Archangel

32. GERANIUM MACRORRHIZUM 'SPESSART'
    Bigroot Geranium

33. PENNISETUM ALOPECUROIDES
    Fountain Grass

34. SEDUM X 'VERA JAMISON'
    Stonecrop

35. MONARDA DIDYMA 'PURPURKRONE'
    Purple Bee Balm

36. ANEMONE HUPEHENSIS 'SEPTEMBER CHARM'
    Pink Japanese Anemone

37. VERONICA LONGIFOLIA 'SUNNY BORDER BLUE'
    Blue Speedwell

38. VERNONIA NOVEBORACENSIS
    New York Ironweed

39. PEROVSKIA ATRIPLICIFOLIA
    Russian Sage

40. CRAMBE CORDIFOLIA
    Colewort

41. SENECIO DORIA
    Groundsel

42. CARYOPTERIS X CLANDONENSIS 'BLUEMIST'
    Bluebeard

43. CHRYSANTHEMUM PACIFICUM
    Gold and Silver Chrysanthemum

44. BRUNNERA MACROPHYLLA
    Siberian Bugloss

45. EUPATORIUM FISTULOSUM 'GATEWAY'
    Joe-Pye Weed

46. MISCANTHUS SINENSIS
    Silver Grass

MISCELLANEOUS

47. RESIDENCE

48. ENTRY DRIVE

49. LILY POND

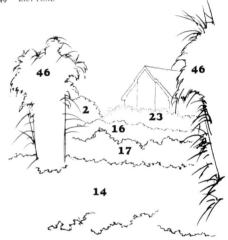

The septic field is planted as a natural garden—a true metaphor for the American meadow.
ROGER FOLEY PHOTOGRAPH

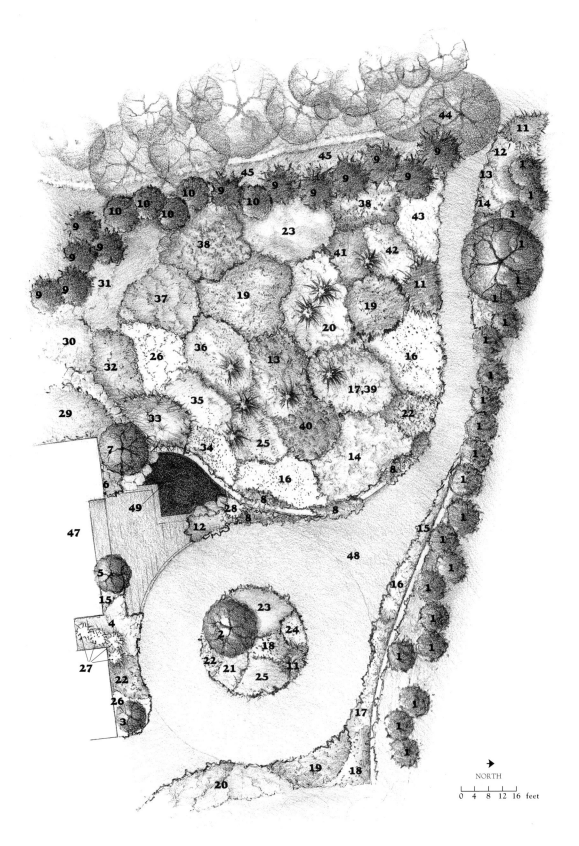

VIRGINIA AVENUE GARDENS OF THE FEDERAL RESERVE SYSTEM

I think Jim's and Wolfgang's work is a natural for the average gardener, particularly their use of perennials. Anyone who really wants to have a garden to enjoy, especially if they are caring for it themselves, understands how important low maintenance is. They have shown the world how to capture the serenity of gardens with very little work.

—DAVID LILLY

Wolfgang and I look back on two seemingly unrelated events of 1977 as landmarks in our partnership. One event was a severe Washington, D.C., winter; the other was an obscure but favorable press review about a Washington garden we had designed.

The severe winter killed most of the regimental evergreens at the Federal Reserve Building. David Lilly, then a member of the Federal Reserve Board of Governors and an accomplished gardener, liked what he saw in the newspaper clipping and decided to contact us. He asked if we could apply similar concepts to redesigning and relandscaping the grounds. It was our first major commission. Little did he know that our "office" at the time was a drafting table in a bedroom of my town house and an aging Volkswagen Squareback stocked with mulch, tools, and potted shrubs. Later, Mr. Lilly told us jokingly, "I knew you had good taste—you plant witch hazel in your gardens!"

The two-acre public garden appears at grade level but is actually constructed on the roof of an underground parking garage. The structure allowed about eighteen inches of soil for planting perennials and lawn and four-foot mounds for trees.

We reclaimed the space around the building for its occupants by placing higher plants near the street. Even in the middle of the city, sweeps of perennials create a lush meadowlike environment. Medium-sized trees offer shade and give context to the monumental scale of the building. Open "rooms," sheltered by plants and embellished with sculpture, attract visitors for strolls, picnics, and reading. It is, in a sense, a neighborhood park.

After the first growing season, we were invited back for a lecture tour of the garden. The staff told us to expect about forty people. We—and they—hardly knew what to do when four hundred showed up! Employees wanted to know more about the garden that they had derided as a patch of weeds when it was first planted. Now they were believers, and they wanted to apply the same principles to their own suburban gardens or in-town balconies.

*My garden is an environment of serenity with
a fascinating variety of forms and textures.
From the time we planted the garden it changed
my life. The garden is as much a part of
my house as any room.*

—PAULINE VOLLMER

THE LEO AND PAULINE VOLLMER GARDEN

Wolfgang began planting this garden in 1962, long before we formed a partnership. The colonial-style house faces north on a typical half-acre suburban lot. The building contractor had planted evergreen shrubs against the foundation of the house in front. Wolfgang especially remembers the spreading *Taxus* sp. (yew) that had been placed carefully under each bay window. They had been chopped into ugly shapes to keep them from covering up the windows. L-shaped beds of *Rosa* spp. (rose) bisected the backyard, and the nondescript lawn completed the original landscaping effort.

Mrs. Vollmer remembers the early rough plans for the garden that Wolfgang showed her and a list of plants that were totally unrecognizable to her and her suburban garden club members. She is amazed today that she and her husband were adventuresome enough to forge ahead.

First, Wolfgang removed two-thirds of the backyard lawn and laid out broad peren-nial planting areas into which he transplanted the *Rosa* spp. He added *Calluna vulgaris* (Scotch heather), *Spodiopogon sibiricus, Brunnera macrophylla,* and *Festuca glauca* (blue fes-cue). He also gave density to the existing screening along the property line with *Pinus thunbergiana* (Japanese black pine) and *Tsuga canadensis* (Canadian hemlock). The Vollmers lived with this part of the garden for a season, decided they liked what was happening, and asked Wolfgang to begin work on the front yard.

In deference to the neighbors he kept lawn on either side of the serpentine walk to the front door. He moved the existing "foundation" shrubs toward the street for privacy and added *Ilex pedunculosa* (longstock holly), *Amelanchier canadensis, Hamamelis mollis* 'Brevipetala' (Chinese witch hazel), and *Corylopsis pauciflora* (buttercup winter haze). Finally, he planted the ground plane using a perennial palette of *Lysimachia punctata* (yellow gooseneck), *Epimedium* spp. (barrenwort), *Helleborus* spp. (lenten rose), and *Hosta* spp. (plaintain lily).

Removing two-thirds of an American suburban lawn was quite revolutionary in the early 1960s; however, before long the Vollmers asked to have the remaining lawn re-moved and planted with perennials.

Mrs. Vollmer maintains the garden herself, bringing in help only occasionally. As she puts it, "The work keeps me from getting decrepit." She and a helper cut the garden down in the spring, shred the trimmings, and put them down as mulch. She doesn't do much fertilizing because the trimmings make excellent plant food.

*PREVIOUS SPREAD AND OPPOSITE:
A light cover of snow reveals how the
dried winter gardens in front and back
are structured with just the right balance
of evergreen. In front, on the right, the
Hamamelis x intermedia 'Arnold
Promise' (witch hazel) is blooming in the
snow. In back, on the left, the Magnolia
grandiflora (southern magnolia) softens
the corner of the house.*

*RIGHT: The shady summer front garden
is lush and green with Bergenia cordifolia (heartleaf bergenia), Hosta spp. (plantain lily), fern sp., Liriope muscari 'Big
Blue' (lily-turf), Ilex pedunculosa
(longstalk holly), and Fargesia nitida.*
ROGER FOLEY PHOTOGRAPHS

PLANT KEY

TREES AND SHRUBS

1 CARPINUS CAROLINIANA
   American Hornbeam

2 CORNUS KOUSA
   Kousa Dogwood

3 ILEX OPACA
   American Holly

4 ILEX X ATTENUATA 'FOSTERI'
   Foster Holly

5 ILEX PEDUNCULOSA
   Longstalk Holly

6 PINUS ARISTATA
   Bristle-Cone Pine

7 PINUS THUNBERGIANA
   Japanese Black Pine

8 FOTHERGILLA GARDENII
   Dwarf Fothergilla

9 CLERODENDRON TRICHOTOMUM
   FARGESII
   Harlequin Glory-Bower

10 CORNUS FLORIDA
   Flowering Dogwood

11 CUNNINGHAMIA LANCEOLATA
   Common China Fir

12 PINUS STROBUS
   Eastern White Pine

13 FRANKLINIA ALATAMAHA
   Franklin Tree

14 ILEX GLABRA
   Inkberry Holly

15 HAMAMELIS VERNALIS
   Vernal Witch Hazel

16 AESCULUS PARVIFLORA
   Bottlebrush Buckeye

17 ELAEAGNUS UMBELLATA
   Autumn Olive

PERENNIALS AND ORNAMENTAL
GRASSES

18 CERATOSTIGMA PLUMBAGINOIDES
   Leadwort

19 BRUNNERA MACROPHYLLA
   Siberian Bugloss

20 SESLERIA AUTUMNALIS
   Autumn Moor Grass

21 PEUCEDANUM VERTICILLARE
   Hog Fennel

22 COREOPSIS VERTICILLATA 'MOONBEAM'
   Cutleaf Tickseed

23 PHYSOSTEGIA VIRGINIANA 'VIVID'
   False Dragonhead

24 LIATRIS SPICATA
   Gayfeather

25 PEROVSKIA ATRIPLICIFOLIA
   Russian Sage

26 MISCANTHUS SINENSIS 'MALEPARTUS'
   Silver Grass

27 TANACETUM MACROPHYLLUM
   Tansy

28 MISCANTHUS SINENSIS GIGANTEUS
   Giant Chinese Silver Grass

29 LAVANDULA ANGUSTIFOLIA 'HIDCOTE'
   Lavender

30 PHLOMIS SAMIA
   Greek Sage

31 CHELONE LYONII
   Turtle-Head

32 FESTUCA GLAUCA
   Blue Fescue

33 PHLOX GLABERRIMA
   Wild Pink Phlox

34 MISCANTHUS SINENSIS 'GRAZIELLA'
   Japanese Maiden Grass

35 ERICA CARNEA
   Snow Heather

36 MACLEAYA CORDATA
   Plume Poppy

37 PENNISETUM ALOPECUROIDES
   Fountain Grass

38 SEDUM X 'AUTUMN JOY'
   Stonecrop

39 YUCCA FILAMENTOSA
   Adam's Needle

40 MISCANTHUS SINENSIS 'GRACILLIMUS'
   Japanese Maiden Grass

41 HYPERICUM CALYCINUM
   St.-John's-Wort

42 RUDBECKIA FULGIDA 'GOLDSTURM'
   Black-eyed Susan

43 SILPHIUM PERFOLIATUM
   Cup Plant

44 CHASMANTHIUM LATIFOLIUM
   Wild Oats

45 CHRYSANTHEMUM PACIFICUM
   Gold and Silver Chrysanthemum

46 CALLUNA VULGARIS
   Scotch Heather

47 CALAMAGROSTIS ACUTIFLORA STRICTA
   Feather Reed Grass

48 CAREX PENDULA
   Drooping Sedge

49 LAMIUM GALEOBDOLON
   Yellow Archangel

50 SALVIA SUPERBA 'MAINACHT'
   Sage

51 AGAPANTHUS UMBELLATUS 'BLUE
   TRIUMPHATOR'
   Lily of the Nile

52 CAREX MORROWII VARIEGATA
   Variegated Japanese Sedge

53 ACHILLEA FILIPENDULA 'MOONSHINE'
   Yarrow

54 EUPATORIUM FISTULOSUM 'GATEWAY'
   Joe-Pye Weed

55 HOSTA SIEBOLDIANA
   Plantain Lily

56 CASSIA MARILANDICA
   Wild Senna

57 LYTHRUM SALICARIA 'MORDEN'S PINK'
   Loosestrife

58 CHRYSANTHEMUM SPP.
   Chrysanthemum

MISCELLANEOUS

59 TERRACE

60 GARDEN WALK

61 FENCE

The meadowlike, sunny back garden in summer.
ROGER FOLEY PHOTOGRAPH

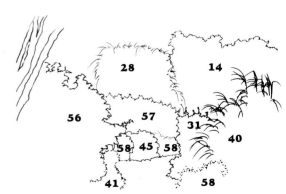

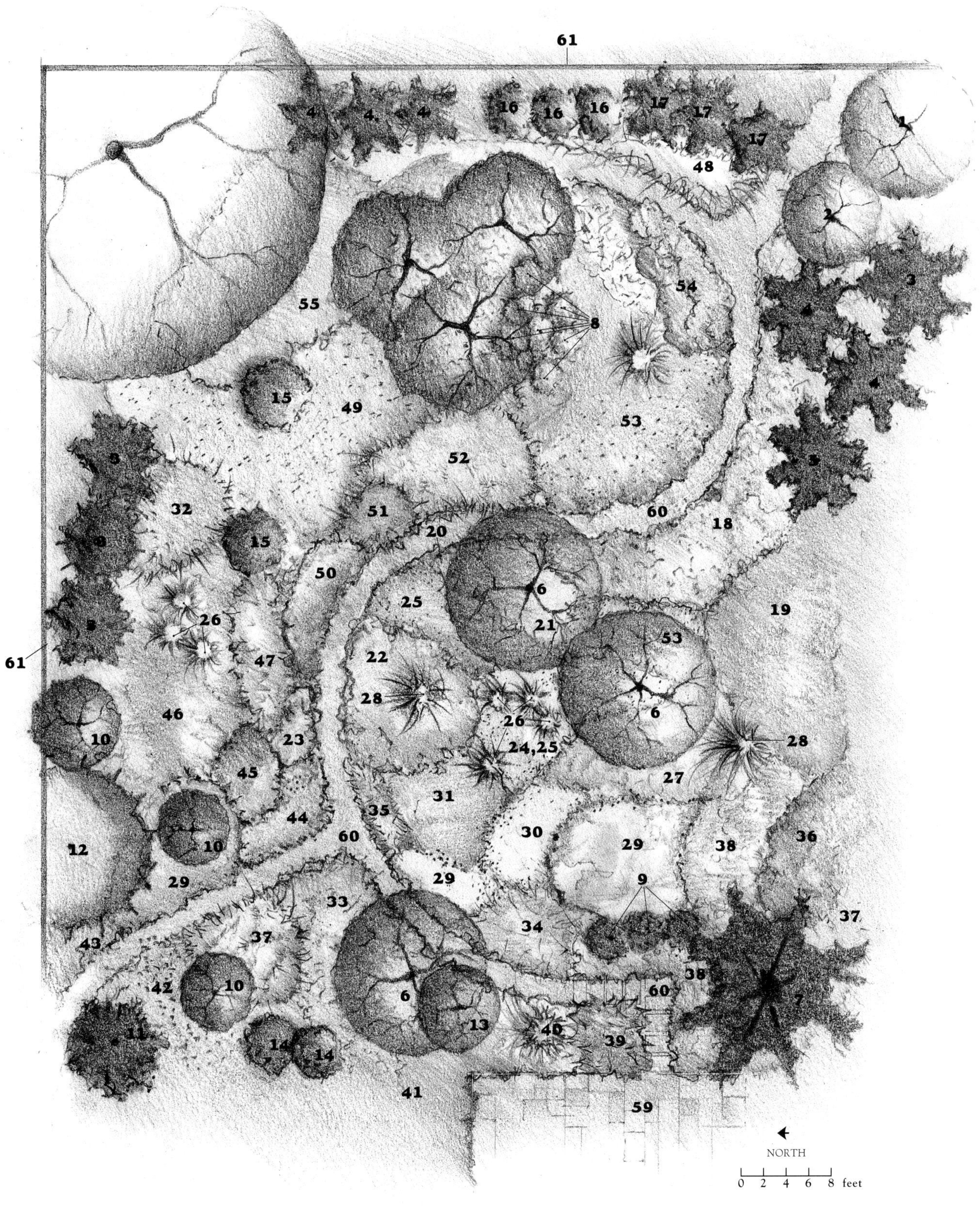

61

4   4   4   16   16   16   17   17   1

17

48   2

3

55   54

15   8

49   53

52

5   60   18

32   51   20

15   50   25   6

26   47   22   21   53

28   26   19

46   23   24,25   28

10   45   31   27

44   60   30   29   38   36

12   10   35   29   9   37

29   33   34   38

43   37   60   7

42   10   6   13   40   39

11   14   14   41   59

NORTH

0 2 4 6 8 feet

Parking garages, like politicians, are often indispensable but rarely esteemed. The unloved stepchildren of an autocentric age, these vast expanses of often sterile and featureless concrete seem to embody the essentially antinature nature of cars. But across the Potomac River from the Capital Mall at Washington National Airport is a notable exception—a parking garage that embraces rather than displaces nature.

—ALICIA RODRIGUEZ, *LANDSCAPE ARCHITECTURE*, FEBRUARY 1996

WASHINGTON NATIONAL AIRPORT SOUTH PARKING GARAGE

N ational Airport's South Parking Garage is a prominent gateway to Washington, D.C. Thousands of people move through and around it each day on foot or in cars, buses, taxis, and the elevated Metrorail. To match the dynamics of the place and add a welcoming touch of softness and nature, we wanted to design a garden that is painterly, dramatic, and jazzy.

We envisioned the garage as a hillside created by complex yet orderly layers of forms, textures, and colors. When we started work I remembered a garage and bus station I saw in Nice, France, several years before. When I had first approached it I was aware only of a great mound of plants, the equivalent of four stories high and five city blocks long. Under the mound I discovered a bus garage on the ground floor and cars parked on multiple decks above. Of course, Nice's semi-tropical climate made the planting task much easier. For National Airport, the challenge was to design, grow, and maintain a year-round container garden of sufficient fullness to disguise the massive building.

We worked closely with the building's architects from the beginning to design and detail the planters properly. The containers are large enough for trees—six feet wide, ten feet long, and five feet deep. They are insulated, automatically irrigated, and drain into the airport's storm system through soil-separating fabric.

The planters define the outside edge of the building on three floors. We planted the largest planters with *Acer ginnala* (amur maple), *Cornus mas* (Cornelian cherry), and *Cotinus coggygria* (smoke tree). We chose plants that cascade over the edge such as *Jasminum nudiflorum* (winter jasmine), *Lamium galeobdolon* (yellow archangel), *Rosa* 'Bonica' and 'Ferdy' (meidiland roses), and *Stranvaesia davidiana* 'Prostrata' (Chinese stranvaesia). The American native grass, *Panicum virgatum,* and the pink *Rosa* 'Bonica' planted on top are beautiful against a blue sky. *Miscanthus sinensis* 'Gracillimus' planted in rectangular blocks resembles giant paintbrushes. The grasses soften the edges, sway in the breezes, and give the entire composition a lively quality.

After four years, the parking garage structure has almost disappeared. The lush combination of trees and cascading plants creates the effect we planned for this busy place—a cross between a hanging garden and a country hillside.

PLANT KEY

TREES AND SHRUBS

1   COTINUS COGGYGRIA
    Smoke Tree
2   ROSA 'FERDY'
    Meidiland Ferdy Rose
3   KERRIA JAPONICA
    Japanese Kerria
4   TAXUS BACCATA 'REPANDENS'
    Spreading English Yew
5   FORSYTHIA X INTERMEDIA 'SPRING GLORY'
    Spring Glory Forsythia
6   ACER GINNALA
    Amur Maple
7   ARCTOSTAPHYLOS UVA-URSI
    Bearberry
8   CORNUS MAS
    Cornelian Cherry
9   JASMINUM NUDIFLORUM
    Winter Jasmine
10 ROSA 'BONICA'
    Meidiland Bonica Rose
11 EUONYMUS ALATUS 'RUDY HAAG'
    Winged Euonymus
12 STRANVAESIA DAVIDIANA UNDULATA
    Chinese Stranvaesia
13 ILEX VERTICILLATA 'SPARKLEBERRY'
    Winterberry Holly
14 QUERCUS PHELLOS
    Willow Oak
15 BETULA NIGRA
    River Birch
16 METASEQUOIA GLYPTOSTROBOIDES
    Dawn Redwood
17 GLEDITSIA TRIACANTHOS INERMIS 'SHADEMASTER'
    Honey Locust

PERENNIALS AND ORNAMENTAL GRASSES

18 PENNISETUM ALOPECUROIDES
    Fountain Grass
19 LIRIOPE MUSCARI 'BIG BLUE'
    Lily-Turf
20 PEROVSKIA ATRIPLICIFOLIA
    Russian Sage
21 PANICUM VIRGATUM 'HAENSE HERMS'
    Red Switch Grass
22 HYPERICUM CALYCINUM
    St.-John's-Wort
23 SARCOCOCCA HOOKERANA
    Himalayan Sarcococca, or Sweetbox
24 POLYGONUM CUSPIDATUM COMPACTUM
    Dwarf Fleece Flower
25 CERATOSTIGMA PLUMBAGINOIDES
    Leadwort
26 SYMPHORICARPOS X CHENAULTI 'HANCOCK'
    Chenault Coralberry
27 MISCANTHUS SINENSIS PURPURASCENS
    Red Maiden Grass
28 ACHILLEA FILIPENDULINA 'CORONATION GOLD'
    Coronation Gold Yarrow
29 YUCCA FILAMENTOSA
    Adam's Needle

MISCELLANEOUS

30 LAWN
31 ENTRY TO PARKING DECK
32 PARKING DECK

PREVIOUS SPREAD AND RIGHT: *The combination of trees, shrubs, and cascading plants is painterly and jazzy. After three years the building is beginning to disappear under planting that is reminiscent of the fabled hanging gardens of Babylon.*
ROGER FOLEY PHOTOGRAPHS

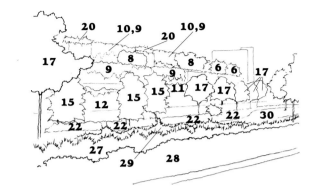

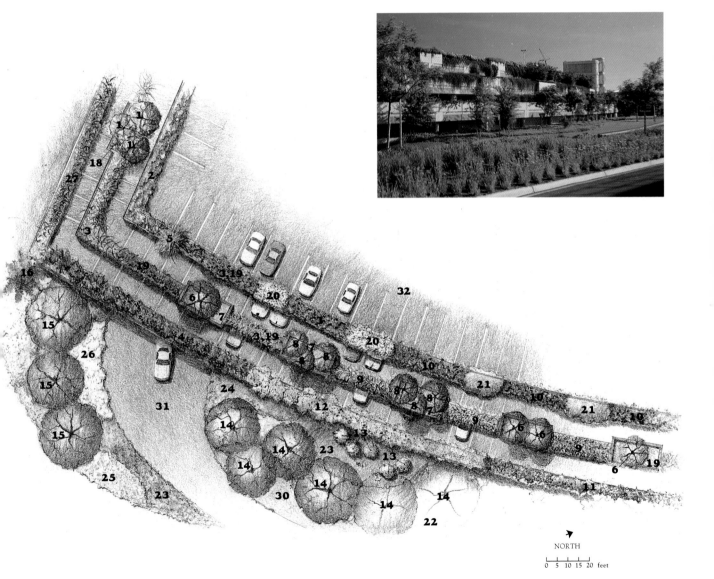

NORTH

0 5 10 15 20 feet

PART III

PLANTING YOUR GARDEN
STEP-BY-STEP

ow I want to shift the emphasis from our gardens to yours by showing you how to create your own New American Garden. The straightforward approach that Wolfgang and I follow is easily adaptable to your garden space. It starts with a basic drawing and proceeds through garden design, planting, and maintenance.

Before starting a planting plan you will need to find or prepare an accurate base drawing that shows your property's boundaries and the locations of its main features. It's best to have a survey of the property. You may find one among real estate closing documents or plans for past construction work. If you don't have a survey, I would recommend that you have one prepared by a professional land surveyor or engineer. The survey drawing will be to scale and will show property boundaries, an outline of the house and other buildings, and the location of permanent site features such as paved areas, walls, fences, and important trees and shrubs. It may also show topographic contour lines (or spot elevations) and the locations of easements and underground utilities. (See below.)

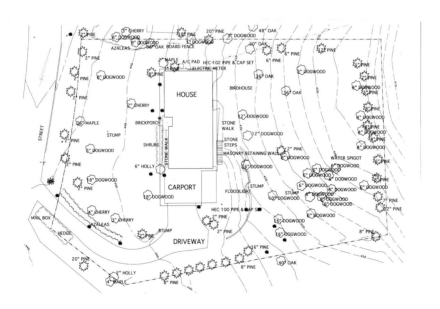

If you don't have a survey you can measure the garden and create a suitable base drawing yourself. If you do it yourself, it is important to be accurate. Go slowly, making sure to locate all the major site features, even those that you may want to remove or relocate later. Use a measuring tape to locate natural features such as rock outcroppings, built features such as retaining walls, and utilities such as drains, water spigots, and electric service. Be sure to show the locations and sizes of all windows and doors that open to the garden. The indoor-outdoor aspect of your design is very important, and you don't want to place taller plants where they will obscure important views. Show all the information accurately on the drawing, using whatever symbols or notations are clear to you. If drainage is an issue (and it usually is), you can even measure approximate changes in ground elevation from point to point by using a long board and a level.

Make several prints of your finished base drawing for taking notes and sketching plans.

EVALUATE YOUR PROPERTY

When Wolfgang and I start a new project we get to know the property as quickly and thoroughly as possible. You must do the same by looking afresh at your garden space. Walk the site, observing existing natural conditions and other features that might enhance or detract from the beauty of your design or influence plant choice. Have a clipboard and camera handy to record your findings and first impressions. The clipboard should have a notepad and a copy of the survey drawing.

Identify problem areas that require special attention, such as steep topography or poor drainage. Then note all existing plants that might be kept or relocated, areas subject to extremes of light and shade, and the garden's orientation to sun and breezes. Also look for special opportunities that might be used to advantage, including "borrowed" off-site scenery—a forest edge, a water feature, a golf course, or even a nearby specimen tree. Note the locations from which unwanted views must be screened out by plantings or by other means. Be sure to look at the garden from inside the house; views from the house may influence the placement of specimen plants or other garden features for year-round enjoyment. Try to imagine what happens to the garden as the seasons progress—how changes in the sun's position affect light and shade, which trees lose their leaves in winter, and where the spring-blooming bulbs will be concentrated.

The photographs you take during the initial reconnaissance will be invaluable references for drawing your planting scheme. They should also be kept as part of a collection that tracks your garden's entire development.

As part of your garden evaluation process it is important to have the soil tested in several places. Soils vary greatly from place to place and might even vary within your garden. Knowledge of the acidity or alkalinity of your soil is essential. You can get a clue to soil types from plants already existing on the site. For example, if your soil is acid you may see *Rhododendron* spp., and if alkaline, *Viburnum* spp. Ferns may indicate that the soil is wet, while *Aster* spp. will indicate dryness. Also, the condition of the plants will help you determine if the soil is too wet or too dry. However, to be accurate, have your soil analyzed professionally. Among other important factors, the tests will show the amount of acidity or alkalinity on a sliding scale known as the pH value. A neutral reading is pH 7. The soil is more alkaline as the reading goes up and more acid as it goes down. The tests should also tell you how much organic matter is present. This information is invaluable both for designing your garden and for preparing the soil properly. Cooperative extension offices in most states will provide this service, usually at a nominal cost. If you need additional help in interpreting the tests, contact your local nursery.

CREATE A PLANTING SCHEME

Start work on your planting scheme by listing your garden requirements. Do you want the planting to be natural and relaxed or more structured and formal? Do you need a lawn space for children to play? List your favorite plants. Are native plants important to you? Do you want a vegetable, cut-flower, or herb garden? Do you have enough space for a meadow? Do you require screening for privacy or stabilizing a slope? Do you want an instant garden or are you patient enough to watch the garden mature slowly? Finally, and most important, what purpose do you want your garden to serve? Will you enjoy doing the work of maintaining your garden yourself? Or is your enjoyment more passive, as viewed from the house or terrace? Will the space be used for entertainment and outdoor living? All of these considerations will influence the garden's style and how it will look.

Let me now share with you some basic tenets of garden design I have arrived at over the years that will help you achieve these objectives. Wolfgang and I rely on design tools such as those listed below when we start to lay out a garden. You will recognize some of them from descriptions in the "Portfolio of Gardens," and you may want to refer back to examples that are particularly relevant.

❑ Establish a garden style. In addition to personal preference and lifestyle, factors that may influence your selection of a style include the architecture of the house and existing garden features that you want to keep. Remember that geometric shapes, straight lines, right angles, and strong axes are more formal in appearance, whereas curvilinear lines, free-form groupings, asymmetric patterns, and soft edges are more relaxed and informal.

❑ Think of your plan in three dimensions. Try to envision the plants' height and mass as you sketch them, and keep in mind that plants grow; your sketches should represent them in their mature state. If your garden space is flat, use plant masses of varying heights to give it three-dimensional interest.

- Play with spatial perception. You can expand or compress your perception of space through plant groupings, tree canopies, reflections on water surfaces, light and shade contrasts, and framing of distant views. Remember that linear patterns leading away from the eye stretch the space and make it look longer and narrower, whereas cross patterns foreshorten the space. Similarly, soft planting edges that blend with foliage on adjacent properties create an illusion of greater space.

- Take advantage of existing slopes. An upward-sloping garden has the drama of a raked stage, whereas a downward-sloping garden does not reveal its mysteries until visitors walk through it and then look back from below. Plants with deep, fibrous roots such as *Rhus aromatica, Campsis radicans, Ceratostigma plumbaginoides, Hypericum calycinum, Carex muskingumensis* (palm sedge), and *Sesleria autumnalis* (autumn moor grass) are best for steep slopes. Heavy mulching may be necessary until the plants are established.

- Set up a progression of views. If you are fortunate enough to have a pleasing distant view, make it part of your garden. Think in terms of foreground, background, and even middle ground. Exaggerate a favorite view by framing it with plants or a structure such as an arbor.

- Never compete with natural beauty. If your garden is surrounded by dramatic natural scenery, keep your planting scheme simple. Use fewer varieties and larger masses; select textures and colors that are sympathetic with the background.

- Don't show everything at once; let your garden unfold as a series of discoveries. Even in a small garden, a meandering path that disappears behind plantings or a low wall entices visitors to investigate what lies beyond.

- If part of your garden is used for entertaining, consider the "outdoor room" concept. Your outdoor room can have "walls" (either plants or built features), a "carpet" (lawn or pavers), and a "ceiling" (tree canopy or vine-covered arbor).

- Reclaim the front yard for yourself. Be selfish with your view by placing the taller plant masses toward the street. Avoid "foundation" planting.

- Use patterns of sun and shade as part of your design. For example, it's always a delight when walking through a shady part of the garden to come upon an unexpected spot of brilliant sunlight.

- Use lawn and paved surfaces advisedly and only for specific purposes. Wolfgang and I limit lawn to functional roles: as an informal circulation system, as a good surface for yard games and children's play, and as a "carpet" for outdoor rooms.

With these thoughts in mind, and your survey drawing, evaluation notes, list of requirements, and photographs in hand, you are ready to start designing. Get a big roll of inexpensive tracing paper and plenty of fat pencils with soft lead. Roll the paper out over the survey drawing, and start drawing loose, freehand sketches. At this stage I like to say I am drawing at arm's length. (See below.) Don't be afraid to use lots of paper, and don't be discouraged if you don't find instant answers. Often I make as many as eight or ten rough sketches before good ideas start to emerge. Keep the big picture in mind—don't try to resolve all the details as you go along; they will be easy and fun to deal with once you have a schematic design.

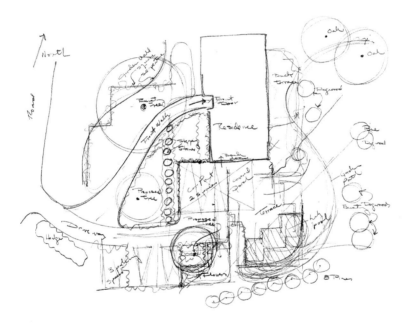

If your new garden will have "hardscape" features, such as walls, steps, paved areas, and pools, sketch them in first.* These are the "bones" of the garden that define residual planting spaces. Then start drawing rough outlines of the plants: sketch in trees and shrubs first to establish the garden's major spatial structure. After these elements are entered, sketch the areas devoted to perennials and lawn. Show only schematic planting areas at this stage—no plant names. Throw away the sketches you don't like, but keep the ones that you may want to refer to later. (See Alternates on facing page.) Your final plan will be a composite of many ideas and sketches.

* For further information on garden pools and other water features, see James van Sweden, *Gardening with Water* (Random House, 1995).

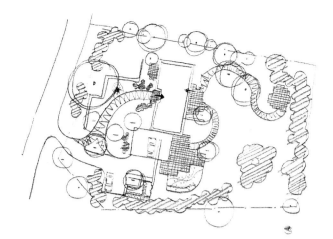

ALTERNATE 1

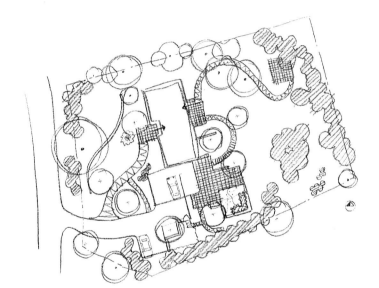

ALTERNATE 2

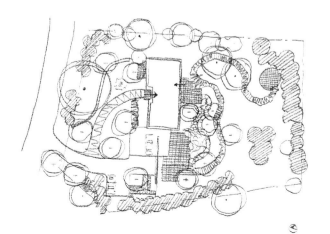

ALTERNATE 3

Once you have selected a preferred schematic design (I chose Alternate 3 in this example), it is time to choose plants from your list and draw the planting scheme. (See below.) At this point you will have decided which existing small trees, shrubs, and perennials you will keep in place, which ones you will transplant, and which ones you will discard (friends are always eager to take unwanted plants). Draw in and name the large trees first, then the small trees and shrubs, and finally the perennials and lawn. This is where I turn the design over to Wolfgang. Notice how his perennial scheme covers the entire ground plane and resembles a patchwork quilt, with large clusters of each variety. If you have the space, don't forget to think in terms of giant sweeps of color.

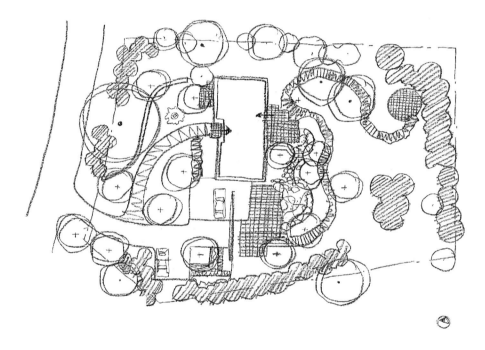

Now you can draw the "hard-line" planting scheme that will guide (but not dictate) the planting of your garden. (See opposite page.) It is also suitable for estimating costs. The final plan will not crystallize, however, until the day you lay out all the plants on the ground. Let your intuition guide you throughout the planting process, and don't be afraid to make changes in your plans as you go along. After all the plants have been placed and while they are still in their pots, take one last look and make final adjustments. When you finish planting, update your drawing by indicating where you have actually placed each plant in the ground. Now you have a final "as planted" plan for your records and it's time to switch hats: you're ready for the pleasures of nurturing and watching your garden evolve over time.

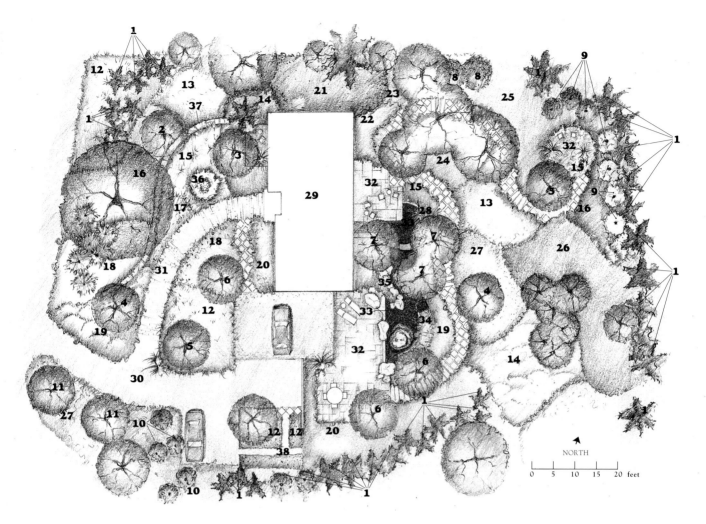

PLANT KEY

TREES AND SHRUBS

1 ILEX X 'NELLIE R. STEVENS'
Nellie R. Stevens Holly

2 CLERODENDRON TRICHOTOMUM FARGESII
Harlequin Glorybower

3 HAMAMELIS X INTERMEDIA 'ARNOLD PROMISE'
Chinese Witch Hazel

4 CHIONANTHUS RETUSUS
Chinese Fringe Tree

5 SYRINGA RETICULATA
Japanese Tree Lilac

6 MAGNOLIA VIRGINIANA
Sweet Bay Magnolia

7 VIBURNUM SIEBOLDII
Siebold Viburnum

8 HYDRANGEA PANICULATA 'TARDIVA'
Panicle Hydrangea

9 HYDRANGEA QUERCIFOLIA
Oakleaf Hydrangea

10 VIBURNUM X PRAGENSE
Prague Viburnum

11 CORNUS KOUSA
Kousa Dogwood

PERENNIALS AND ORNAMENTAL GRASSES

12 LIRIOPE MUSCARI 'BIG BLUE'
Lily-Turf

13 TANACETUM MACROPHYLLUM
Tansy Daisy

14 POLYGONUM AMPLEXICAULE 'FIRETAIL'
Fleece Flower

15 HAKONECHLOA MACRA
Hakone Grass

16 HEUCHERA VILLOSA
Coral Bells

17 EPIMEDIUM PERRALDERIANUM 'FROHNLEITEN'
Barrenwort

18 GERANIUM MACRORRHIZUM
Bigroot Geranium

19 EUPHORBIA AMYGDALOIDES 'ROBBIAE'
Wood Spurge

20 BEGONIA GRANDIS
Hardy Pink Begonia

21 ARALIA CORDATA
Japanese Spikenard

22 BRUNNERA MACROPHYLLA
Siberian Bugloss

23 LIGULARIA DENTATA 'DESDEMONA'
Bigleaf Goldenray

24 HOSTA 'SUM AND SUBSTANCE'
Plantain Lily

25 ANEMONE JAPONICA 'HONORINE JOBERT'
Dark Pink Japanese Anemone

26 LYSIMACHIA CLETHROIDES
Gooseneck Loosestrife

27 SENECIO AUREUS
Golden Groundsel

AQUATICS

28 THALIA DEALBATA
Hardy Water Canna

MISCELLANEOUS

29 RESIDENCE

30 ENTRY DRIVE

31 ENTRY WALK

32 STONE TERRACE

33 LILY POND

34 AQUATIC PLANTER

35 WATERFALL

36 WATER FEATURE

37 STONE RETAINING WALL

38 VEGETABLE AND HERB GARDEN

The key to successfully planting your garden is the proper sequencing of tasks. On the basis of our experience with many types and sizes of gardens, Wolfgang and I have developed an effective step-by-step program that we follow religiously.

STEP ONE: Have all the underground utilities on your property flagged by the respective utility companies. It's important to locate them all: gas, electric, telephone, sewer, and any other service lines. Check carefully for all approvals and permits that may be required in your jurisdiction. Secure and post the various building permits. Remember that every jurisdiction is different. For instance, if you are adding electric lines for garden lighting, a permit is usually required. To get the permit you probably will need a stamped drawing prepared by a licensed electrician. Also, some neighborhoods require that you get approval before removing trees that are larger than a specified size. If the ground on a slope is to be disturbed, you may find that you have to place bales of hay or other barriers along the bottom of the slope to inhibit water runoff, catch silt, and prevent erosion.

STEP TWO: Tag all existing large trees, separating those you want to retain from those you will cut down. Move all existing shrubs, small trees, and perennials that you have decided to keep to a holding area and heel them in for planting later. Give away and discard unwanted plants. Now cut down the large trees that you will not be using in your new garden.

STEP THREE: Lay out the shapes of the planting areas shown on your planting scheme using stakes, a garden hose, or fluorescent spray paint. Adjust the shapes to satisfy any special field conditions or new inspirations that might occur to you on the spot. I find that subtle last-minute changes are always required in the field when I survey the planting area from eye level.

STEP FOUR: When you have the perimeters of the planting areas laid out on the ground, remove any existing sod or weeds from within their boundaries. If possible, compost the unwanted sod for at least one year. It will be invaluable as humus when added to the garden later during routine maintenance.

STEP FIVE: If you need to make grading adjustments in your planting areas you should do it now. For example, you may want to create a berm or correct a drainage problem.

STEP SIX: Plant large trees that require heavy equipment such as a cart, a front-end loader, or a tree spade. Be sure the trees are planted three to four inches above the surface of the planting area or "high in the ground." Also, check that they are perfectly vertical and that their best sides face forward. Stake trees firmly for the first year to guard against toppling in the event of high winds.

STEP SEVEN: Prepare the soil by rototilling to a depth of eight to twelve inches, and add the amendments recommended as a result of your soil tests.

STEP EIGHT: Trench and place underground lines for irrigation and site lighting. With the large trees in place, you can easily trench without disturbing them.

STEP NINE: After the underground lines are in place and the grading is fine-tuned, spread two inches of mulch over the entire area to be planted. We use mulch to keep weeds down, hold moisture, and give the beds a finished look. Mulch also breaks down over time, adding humus to the soil. Our preference is for shredded hardwood; however, pine needles, composted sod, and shredded dried perennials from the winter garden also are acceptable. I especially like the fragrance of freshly laid hardwood mulch.

STEP TEN: Lay out and adjust the shrubs and small trees. I find this to be a crucial moment of decision making, because a misplaced tree may block a window or spoil a perfectly framed view if planted exactly as shown on the drawing. A slight adjustment to the left or right sometimes makes all the difference. Just as with the large trees, it is important to carefully rotate the small trees and shrubs to show off their best sides. Also be sure that they are perfectly vertical and that the top of the ball is set two or three inches above the ground.

STEP ELEVEN: Lay out all of the pots of perennials in each planting area at once so you can visualize the design as a whole. After you have made adjustments, remove each plant from the pot and plant it in the ground (see photograph, above).

STEP TWELVE: Top-dress all planting areas with a little more mulch to make them look perfect. Make sure to pull mulch away from tree trunks. Mulch will keep the bark of the tree too moist, block air circulation, and harbor insects. Finally, water each plant by hand thoroughly.

ESTABLISH AND MAINTAIN YOUR GARDEN

Once the construction and planting of your garden is complete, maintenance activities begin. These activities are both pleasurable and good exercise. Watching the garden's initial grow-in is very satisfying. With a modest amount of work you will be amazed at your success.

First, make sure the newly planted perennials have plenty of water for at least a month after planting. Some hand watering may be necessary, even if you have an automatic irrigation system. Once the plants are well established you can cut back to a normal schedule of watering. In your enthusiasm, be careful not to water too much. If you find standing water or signs that the soil is unduly wet, adjust your irrigation system to reduce the watering schedule. If that doesn't work, check for improper drainage. It may be necessary to make drainage adjustments.

To achieve full cover in perennial areas we think it's good practice to replace dead or declining plants as they appear. Also, watch for weeds that may emerge during the initial period of growth and remove them promptly, preferably by hand. (Wolfgang views weeding as a kind of meditation.) Weeds will grow until the new plants shade out the ground surface. This means your garden will take

ABOVE: *One of the photographs of the Carole and Alex Rosenberg garden on Mecox Bay, Long Island, that inspired the planting design of the Nelson A. Rockefeller Park in New York City (see page 123).*

a little extra weeding for the first year or two. We discourage the use of pesticides and herbicides.

Trees and shrubs take longer to become established—up to three years or more. Watch your newly planted trees for signs of decline. Again, hand watering may be required, especially during long periods of hot, dry weather; however, be careful not to overwater. Unlike perennials, which can be replaced at any time, trees should be replaced in the fall or spring, but never during periods of extreme temperature or drought.

Remember when pruning your trees and shrubs to study carefully the habit of the tree or shrub so you can help it achieve its most beautiful and natural-looking form. Wolfgang and I never carve plants into unnatural shapes but let them grow naturally. But we do give them a little help along the way.

In exchange for year-round pleasure, your established garden will require some attention during each season. Although our gardens are low maintenance, no garden is maintenance free. My grandfather had the fantasy of paving over his lot with green concrete. Even that would require sweeping.

The following is a summary of what to expect and what to do during each season, beginning with spring:

Spring: Cut back, remove, and compost the dried perennials and grasses in early spring or late winter, just before the bulbs begin to poke through. Add mulch where necessary. Check for early-growing weeds, such as chickweed. When the risk of frost has passed, plant annuals in your terrace containers and planters.

Summer: Keep an eye out for weeds and remove them as you walk through your planting areas. Water by hand as necessary.

Fall: Plant the spring-blooming bulbs among late-growing grasses and perennials, such as *Pennisetum alopecuroides* and *Rudbeckia fulgida* 'Goldsturm' (see photograph above). Place them between plants and put several in a hole or broadcast them over a large area and plant them where they fall. Do not cut back the dried perennials now, because they make the winter garden beautiful and provide food and give cover to birds and other wildlife. Prune your trees and shrubs as necessary.

Winter: The maintenance year is over. Now sit back and enjoy the beautiful "dried bouquet" of your winter garden until it's time to cut back the dried perennials and grasses. Then the bulbs can take over and start a glorious new garden cycle.

PART IV

FAVORITE PLANTS

Wolfgang is a consummate plantsperson. His knowledge of perennials, grasses and sedges, and vines is key to our successful garden design. He is always on the lookout for plants that meet our requirements for toughness, versatility, seasonal variation, color, and form. This section of the book is a selected list of proven performers that meet our criteria. The list is based on our practical experience with different climatic zones and garden situations.

Most descriptions are cross-referenced to a page in the "Portfolio of Gardens" chapter, in Part II, that shows the plant in a garden setting and in different seasons. The plants are divided into three categories: perennials, grasses and sedges, and vines. They are listed alphabetically by their botanical name, made up of genus, species, and, if appropriate, variety.

"Family" relates the plant to its larger category, or "genera," based on similar flowers or fruits. "Native Range" gives its geographical homeland. "USDA Zones" delineates where the plant prefers to grow, as given by the plant-hardiness zone map published by the United States Department of Agriculture. "Type" indicates whether the plant is herbaceous, deciduous, or evergreen. "Height" is given as an average, and "Spacing" is our recommendation in order to avoid overplanting.

"Conditions" under which the plant grows best are described next. Light requirements given here include "partial shade," meaning morning sun and afternoon shade, and "partial sun," meaning morning shade and afternoon sun. Acidity or alkalinity of soil required is vital to the plant's survival. The descriptions also note how special site conditions and problems influence our plant selections. The deer population in some areas is an issue that comes quickly to mind. Since we frequently face the problem of plants being eaten by deer, we indicate which plants we know they may damage. Keep in mind, however, that deer appetites seem to change at a whim. Other examples of site conditions that influence our plant selections are exposure to salt spray (for which we recommend salt-tolerant plants), unstable or disturbed slopes (plants with fibrous root systems), and arid soils (drought-tolerant plants). Many of the perennials and grasses that we use are natives and are well adapted to dry, exposed conditions.

The categories of "Characteristics" and "Use" are described in a single paragraph. "Characteristics" are described by several terms. A "drupe" is a fleshy fruit containing a hard-coated seed. "Inflorescence" refers to a plant's flowering part; an "umbel" is a flat-topped inflorescence with stalks arising from the same point; a loose, long, compound flower-cluster is termed a "panicle." When a plant spreads by means of "rhizomes," it sends out horizontal roots from which new leaves or stems grow. Bloom dates are given by season rather than by month. "Use" suggests various ways that Wolfgang and I like to use the plant in a garden setting—as a single "specimen," in a small "accent" group, along a "planting area" edge, in large "masses," or as a "ground cover." "In association with" lists some plants that we think are most compatible.

We have not included a bulb list because we believe spring is so easy to do. Just broadcast a selection of your favorite bulbs over the planting area, dig them in where they fall, and enjoy a glorious spring. We use wide selections of *Narcissus* spp. because they are reliable, beautiful in the shade, and can be naturalized. However, tulips are the biggest show, and we treat them like annuals to ensure the most exuberant display. To provide several weeks of bloom, we use 'Emperor' in all colors for an early display and the lily-flowering types for later and longer-lasting bloom. My all-time favorite lily flowering tulip is 'Red Shine'. I always plant enough to pick for my house.

Other bulbs that we regularly use include *Allium giganteum* (giant ornamental onion), the blue-spiked *Camassia cusickii* (quamash), and *Fritillaria persica* (Persian fritillary). We plant *Muscari armeniacum* (grape hyacinth) and *Crocus* spp. close up along walks and terraces.

In the sunny parts of my garden I especially like the delicate blue flowers of *Brunnera macrophylla* (Siberian bugloss) and the white flowers of *Mazus reptans* 'Alba' (white mazus) with the lily-flowering tulips and the light blue spikes of *Camassia cusickii*. I enjoy late-blooming *Narcissus* spp., planted in shady areas in combination with *Hosta* spp. and *Ligularia* spp.

In late spring, the Magnolia virginiana *(sweet bay magnolia) in my garden is blooming with fragrant white flowers, the mulch is totally covered by a carpet of perennials, and the* Miscanthus sinensis giganteus *(giant Chinese silver grass) is already four feet high. Notice how I plant annual Lantana cultivars in the pots for bright color.*

PERENNIALS

ACANTHUS HUNGARICUS

Bear's-Breech (*below*)

✌

FAMILY: Acanthaceae
NATIVE RANGE: Southeast Europe
USDA ZONES: 5–9
TYPE: Herbaceous
HEIGHT: 36 inches
SPACING: 24 inches
CONDITIONS: Prefers sun or shade; does best in partial shade as leaves tend to wilt with too

much afternoon sun. Likes well-drained soil; tolerates drought. Responds well to fertilization by producing more flowers. Once *Acanthus* becomes well established in a spot, it's there to stay: if the original plant is moved, new shoots develop from any root segments that may remain. Formerly *A. balcanicus*, *A. hungaricus* is the best flowering *Acanthus* for cooler climates, though it is not evergreen, like *A. mollis*, which prefers warmer regions.

CHARACTERISTICS AND USE: The familiar *Acanthus* leaf is a classic ornamental figure in Western architecture: it's easy to recognize the plant's arching form with its deeply serrate, dark green foliage, and its thistle-like leaves (without the thistle's formidable prickles). *Acanthus* also produces a profusion of handsome, vertical mauve flowers on upright spikes whose distinctive forms remain well into winter. Summer's green leaves dry brown and hang on until the first hard frost. This is a fine choice for use as an accent, but it can also be planted in masses. It's great for dried-flower arrangements. I recommend situating it near *Ceratostigma plumbaginoides*, *Coreopsis* spp., and *Helictotrichon sempervirens* (blue oat grass).

SEE PAGE 2

ACHILLEA FILIPENDULINA

Coronation Gold Yarrow

✌

FAMILY: Compositae
NATIVE RANGE: Asia Minor and Caucasus
USDA ZONES: 4–9
TYPE: Herbaceous
HEIGHT: 36 inches
SPACING: 24 inches
CONDITIONS: Grows best in full sun; prefers well-drained soil of moderate fertility. Drought tolerant; yet does not stand wet soil when dormant. 'Coronation Gold' is one of the best upright yarrow varieties available to date, though others have recently made a stand, like 'Feuerland' and 'Terra Cotta', selected by Ernst Pagels in Leer, Ostfriesland, Germany.

CHARACTERISTICS AND USE: Another mainstay in many of our gardens because of its reliability and interesting foliage and flower. *Achillea*'s fine, feathery, gray-green foliage and flat-topped, golden-yellow flowers look marvelous when massed or included in a perennial border. They also brighten dried-flower arrangements. The foliage tends to be evergreen at its base, and its flowers show up in early summer and stay on through winter, turning brown as they dry. The leaves and flowers pro-

duce an aromatic herbal essence when you dry and crush them. Try planting *Achillea* near *Helenium* spp. (sneezeweed), *Nepeta* spp., *Pennisetum alopecuroides, Rudbeckia* spp., *Salvia nemorosa* (sage), and *Veronica* x 'Goodness Grows' (speedwell).
SEE PAGES 46–47

AMSONIA TABERNAEMONTANA
Blue Star Flower
ꔮꔮꔮ

FAMILY: Apocynaceae
NATIVE RANGE: North America
USDA ZONES: 4–8
TYPE: Herbaceous
HEIGHT: 36 inches
SPACING: 18 inches
CONDITIONS: Prefers dappled shade though does well in sun if given moist soils; clump-forming though slow to get established and growing.
CHARACTERISTICS AND USE: This pretty plant brings forth light blue, star-shaped flowers in late spring and early summer, on stems whorled in narrow, bright green leaves. I like *Amsonia* because it's one of the few herbaceous species whose leaves provide long-lasting fall color: its foliage stays golden until the first frost. A good choice for planting at the woodland edge, alongside a stream, and in other natural settings. It makes a fine cut flower.

ARALIA RACEMOSA
Spikenard (*below*)
ꔮꔮꔮ

FAMILY: Araliaceae
NATIVE RANGE: Eastern North America
USDA ZONES: 4–9
TYPE: Herbaceous
HEIGHT: 4–5 feet
SPACING: 4 feet
CONDITIONS: Prefers fertile soil with sufficient moisture in sun or partial shade. Does best in cool conditions: if too hot, leaves tend to brown-out. *A. cordata* and *A. californica* tend to be more robust and heat tolerant than *A. racemosa*, especially in partial shade; these should not be mistaken for the spiny, tree-form, *A. spinosa*.
CHARACTERISTICS AND USE: *Aralia* is an interesting plant, if a bit finicky. It much prefers a cool summer climate and some shade. Its coarse, broad leaves grow loosely on tall stalks, and by summer, pale white panicles of umbel flowers, tinged with a hint of green, begin to appear. By midseason, the spent flowers begin to yield clusters of small, round, lustrous green fruit. These mature to brown, purple, or black, and their weight pulls at the stems so that they begin to arch gently. *Aralia* is fine as a specimen or for naturalizing. Plant it near *Anemone japonica* (Japanese anemone), *Astilbe* spp. (false spirea), *Geranium macrorrhizum, Hosta* spp., *Lamium galeobdolon* (yellow archangel), *Ligularia dentata,* and various ferns.
SEE PAGE 111

ARTEMISIA
'POWIS CASTLE'
Wormwood

FAMILY: Compositae
NATIVE RANGE: Europe
USDA ZONES: 4–8
TYPE: Herbaceous, though older stems are woody
HEIGHT: 3–4 feet
SPACING: 18 inches
CONDITIONS: Prefers full sun; requires good drainage. Wolfgang recommends "drastic pruning" once every several years to flush out the old stems and rejuvenate new growth, particularly after a cold winter. 'Powis Castle' is a hybrid between *A. arborescens* and *A. absinthium.*
CHARACTERISTICS AND USE: I love *Artemisia*'s finely cut, silvery leaves, which mound in a shrublike form and may, in some warmer regions, stay evergreen. Although this variety rarely blooms in summer, the color and texture of its sparkling, aromatic foliage make it well worth your while. It's excellent for edging, massing, and planting on slopes or among rocks, and I like to see it planted with *Nepeta* spp., and *Sedum* spp. A beautiful texture and color for the garden, with a bit of tantalizing history (and the evocative name to go with it): *Artemisia* is used to produce the liqueur absinthe, among other ancient potions and remedies.
SEE PAGES 120 (below), 134–35

ARUNCUS DIOICUS
Goatsbeard (*below*)

FAMILY: Rosaceae
NATIVE RANGE: Northern Hemisphere: Europe, Asia, and North America
USDA ZONES: 3–9
TYPE: Herbaceous
HEIGHT: 4–6 feet
SPACING: 36 inches
CONDITIONS: Prefers rich, moist soil in partial shade; tolerates afternoon sun in northern reaches.
CHARACTERISTICS AND USE: This pretty, shade-loving plant has a loose habit of arching stalks. Its leaflets are marked by double serrations along their edges. In early summer, soft white panicle flowers appear at the ends of stems, rising above its deep green, compound leaves. The flowers remind me a little of white-flowering *Astilbes*. The male and female plants flower differently from one another: in males, the plumes grow more upright; in females, the weight of seed heads tends to bend them over a little. This is a good plant for massing in the shade, naturalizing, or planting as a specimen, and it's quite compatible with *Astilbe* spp. (false spirea), *Campanula punctata* (bellflower), *Carex pendula* (drooping sedge), and *Symphytum grandiflorum* (comfrey).

ASCLEPIAS TUBEROSA
Butterfly Weed (*opposite*)

FAMILY: Asclepiadaceae
NATIVE RANGE: Eastern and central North America
USDA ZONES: 4–9

TYPE: Herbaceous
HEIGHT: 2–3 feet
SPACING: 24 inches
CONDITIONS: Likes well-drained, sandy soils in full sun; drought tolerant. Slow to establish as tuber roots develop and take hold; difficult to transplant. A recent introduction, 'Gay Butterfly', exhibits a mixture of yellow, orange, and red within the same flower clusters.
CHARACTERISTICS AND USE: A wonderful, multiseasonal plant that produces eye-catching blooms throughout the summer. *Asclepias* forms in clumps with oblong leaves whorled around plump stems. Its radiant orange umbel flowers put on a fiery display that monarch butterflies love. In autumn, its individual pods burst open and release a profuse haze of seeds on shiny, silky hairs, which take flight even in a light breeze. Use this plant for massing, naturalizing, and in sunny meadows. Its flow-

ers' "hot" colors intensify the effect of cut-flower arrangements. I also like to see it planted in association with *Rudbeckia* spp.

ASTER NOVAE-ANGLIAE
New England Aster

FAMILY: Compositae
NATIVE RANGE: Eastern and central United States
USDA ZONES: 4–8
TYPE: Herbaceous
HEIGHT: 3–5 feet
SPACING: 30 inches
CONDITIONS: Does best in sun or partial shade; tolerates wet soils. Wolfgang recommends reducing stems by a third in midsummer to prevent them from flopping over when in full bloom. One of his favorites is 'Alma Poetschke', a beautiful, hot-pink-flowering variety; 'Purple Dome' is a prolific selection, spreading from seeds.

CHARACTERISTICS AND USE: This plant provides a dose of welcome color in late summer and early fall, and I think it complements other flowers well, either in the garden or in cut-flower arrangements. It has a mounding form composed of tough stems and narrow, gray-green leaves. Its flowers are tiny, daisy-like, with bright yellow disks. They bloom in masses from August well into autumn, and their colors—which tend to soften and complement the hotter late-season colors of plants such as *Rudbeckia* spp.—may range from pink to violet, depending on which variety you select. Use this *Aster* for massing and as a cut flower, and try planting it near *Achillea* spp., *Artemesia* spp., *Chrysanthemum* spp., *Pennisetum alopecuroides,* and *Spodiopogon sibericus.*
SEE PAGES 32 (bottom), 141

BOLTONIA ASTEROIDES
Boltonia (page 178)

FAMILY: Compositae
NATIVE RANGE: Eastern and central United States
USDA ZONES: 4–9
TYPE: Herbaceous
HEIGHT: 3–5 feet
SPACING: 30 inches
CONDITIONS: Grows best in sun or partial shade with moist, rich soils; yet is extremely drought tolerant, appearing to

"grow on air," as Wolfgang puts it. 'Snowbank' is an outstanding selection, providing sprays of snow-white blooms from late summer until frost.

CHARACTERISTICS AND USE: This hardy, late-season native bloomer produces many branching stems and narrow gray-green leaves. In late summer, it yields tiny, asterlike flowers with bright yellow centers and white, pink, or lilac petals in billowy arrays. Boltonia looks beautiful in sunny meadows, massed in the garden, and planted in association with *Eupatorium* spp. (joe-pye weed), *Perovskia atriplicifolia*, and *Sedum* x 'Autumn Joy'.
SEE PAGE 72

CARYOPTERIS X *CLANDONENSIS*
Bluebeard
⊷⊶

FAMILY: Verbenaceae
NATIVE RANGE: Japan to northwest China
USDA ZONES: 5–9
TYPE: Woody sub-shrub (typically dies back to the ground each winter; should be treated as an herbaceous perennial)
HEIGHT: 24–30 inches
SPACING: 30 inches
CONDITIONS: Prefers full sun or partial shade in loose, well-drained soil; drought tolerant. Cut back six inches from the ground by late winter to stimulate flowering during the upcoming growing season. 'Dark Knight' produces the deepest blue blooms of present selections.
CHARACTERISTICS AND USE: Another excellent late bloomer, this shrublike perennial grows in a loose form with very attractive gray-green foliage. I particularly like its airy blue flowers, which encircle the current season's growth and attract multitudes of bees and butterflies. They create a late-summer mist of blue, which also softens the hotter, yellow tones of other late-season bloomers. A lovely addition to a seaside garden, this plant is good for massing and may also be situated near *Calamagrostis* spp., *Panicum virgatum*, *Pennisetum alopecuroides*, *Perovskia atriplicifolia*, *Sedum* x 'Autumn Joy', *Spodiopogon sibiricus*, and *Stachys byzantina* (lamb's ears).
SEE PAGES 134–35

CERATOSTIGMA *PLUMBAGINOIDES*
Leadwort
⊷⊶

FAMILY: Plumbaginaceae
NATIVE RANGE: Western China
USDA ZONES: 5–9
TYPE: Herbaceous, though stems have a woody character
HEIGHT: 12 inches
SPACING: 12–18 inches
CONDITIONS: Prefers full sun to partial shade in fertile, well-drained soil; extremely drought tolerant. Provide a light cover of mulch for winter protection in colder zones.
CHARACTERISTICS AND USE: Although it leafs out later in the spring than most perennials, leadwort's foliage and flowers more than make up for it. It produces lovely clusters of periwinkle-like flowers that attract scores of bees and butterflies throughout the summer, and its fresh green foliage turns to a handsome dark red or bronze in the fall. Once established, the plant spreads freely via underground rhizomes. I consider this an outstanding ground cover for hot spots, and it works well when planted with *Coreopsis* spp., *Liriope muscari* (lily-turf), *Panicum virgatum*, *Pennisetum alopecuroides*,

Sedum spp., and *Yucca filamentosa*. I like to plant it alongside crocuses, because it comes in to leaf just as the bulbs fade.
SEE PAGE 142

CHRYSANTHEMUM PACIFICUM

Gold and Silver Chrysanthemum

FAMILY: Compositae
NATIVE RANGE: Japan
USDA ZONES: 6–9
TYPE: Herbaceous
HEIGHT: 24 inches
SPACING: 18–24 inches
CONDITIONS: Likes full sun or partial shade; drought tolerant though prefers moist, rich soils. Needs good drainage, particularly during winter, to prevent die-out.
CHARACTERISTICS AND USE: I love this mounding perennial's distinguished foliage: it has elegant, dark green leaves that appear lobed and light-colored underneath and are edged in white. Each leaf appears to have an inflorescent border. Its flowers are less fine: it has tansy-like blooms consisting of rayless, yellow buttons that grow in clusters. Although they are otherwise undramatic, the blooms hang on from late summer to frost, and they seem to glow against a light dusting of snow. I like to use it for massing or to define an edge. Try situating it near *Miscanthus sinensis giganteus*.
SEE PAGES 23, 49

CIMICIFUGA RACEMOSA

Black Snakeroot (*below*)

FAMILY: Ranunculaceae
NATIVE RANGE: Eastern United States
USDA ZONES: 3–8
TYPE: Herbaceous
HEIGHT: 6–8 feet
SPACING: 30–36 inches
CONDITIONS: Adapted to rich, moist, acid soils in shady spots; drought tolerant once established; often found along woodland edges in the wild.
CHARACTERISTICS AND USE: Here is a noteworthy native with fine, fernlike foliage and hazy white blossoms. Its leaves are interesting, divided intricately in threes and growing sometimes to a foot and a half across. Late-summer spires of fragrant racemes on narrowly branched stems give snakeroot a dramatic profile, and after the flower spikes stop blooming weeks later, they're followed by dark, decorative seeds. Use it for massing or as an accent in the shade garden. I like to see it planted with *Lobelia cardinalis* (cardinal flower).

COREOPSIS VERTICILLATA

Threadleaf Tickseed

FAMILY: Compositae
NATIVE RANGE: Eastern United States
USDA ZONES: 3–9
TYPE: Herbaceous
HEIGHT: 18–24 inches
SPACING: 18–24 inches
CONDITIONS: Performs best in full sun or partial shade; prefers well-drained soils, although tolerates most conditions, including drought. 'Moonbeam' is a popular variety, bearing soft, lemon-yellow flowers from early summer to fall; 'Zagreb' is another notable variety.

CHARACTERISTICS AND USE: One of our favorite plants, with good reason: *C. verticillata*'s fine stems and airy foliage, like narrow green filaments, grow in billowy clumps when massed and send out low starry sweeps of pure yellow, daisy-like flowers in profusion. Later the flowers give way to dark round seeds, which vaguely resemble small bugs or ticks (hence the common name). Although it shows up late in the spring, once reestablished it spreads freely by rhizomes. A wonderful plant for massing and edging or for use in planters or pots. Plant it in association with *Echinacea purpurea*, *Helictotrichon sempervirens* (blue oat grass), *Liatris spicata*, and *Perovskia atriplicifolia*.

SEE PAGE 66

ECHINACEA PURPUREA
Purple Coneflower (*above*)

❧

FAMILY: Compositae
NATIVE RANGE: Eastern and central United States
USDA ZONES: 3–9
TYPE: Herbaceous
HEIGHT: 24–48 inches
SPACING: 24–36 inches
CONDITIONS: Likes full sun to partial shade in well-drained soils; does not benefit from repeat application of supplemental fertilizer. Admirably withstands summer heat; drought tolerant; self-seeds. 'Leuchtstern', a rose-colored, free-flowering variety, is a good performer in most regions.

CHARACTERISTICS AND USE: *E. purpurea* is a hardy prairie perennial with deep green serrate leaves and beautiful bold flowers. Another favorite of butterflies, its flowers' broad petals range in color from pale rose to deep purple and arch back from prominent, bronze-tinted central cones. The colors are both electric and subtle, and it's a generous summer-long bloomer. In autumn its dramatic seed cones darken as they dry, offering food for birds. A good choice for massing, planting in a sunny meadow, naturalizing, or for cut-flower arrangements.

SEE PAGE 26 (bottom)

EPIMEDIUM PERRALDERIANUM
Barrenwort (*opposite*)

❧

FAMILY: Berberidaceae
NATIVE RANGE: Algeria
USDA ZONES: 5–9
TYPE: Herbaceous, though somewhat evergreen
HEIGHT: 12 inches
SPACING: 12–18 inches
CONDITIONS: Partial shade or full sun if given ample moisture. Prefers cool, shady locations and well-drained soils. The German selection 'Frohnleiten' is a compact form with blooms held high above leaves.

CHARACTERISTICS AND USE:
A great plant for massing and
using as ground cover. Plant this
excellent, interesting ground
cover around the bases of trees
and shrubs. Barrenwort, it seems,
is anything but: it is a creeping
semi-evergreen with very attractive, multiseasonal foliage and a
pretty flower to boot. Its glossy,
heart-shaped leaves display varying tones of green. Its new
growth emerges bronze-tinted,

becomes bright green in midsummer, then is tinged with copper
by winter. In early spring, fresh
sprays of dainty yellow flowers
emerge. I recommend planting it
in association with *Anemone
japonica* (Japanese anemone),
Astilbe spp. (false spirea), *Bergenia
cordifolia* (heartleaf bergenia),
Euphorbia amygdaloides robbiae
(spurge), *Geranium macrorrhizum,*
and *Symphytum grandiflorum*
(comfrey).

*GERANIUM
MACRORRHIZUM*
Bigroot Geranium

FAMILY: Geraniaceae
NATIVE RANGE: Southern
Europe
USDA ZONES: 4–9
TYPE: Herbaceous, yet semi-
evergreen with somewhat
woody stems
HEIGHT: 12–18 inches

SPACING: 18 inches
CONDITIONS: Does best in full or partial shade, growing freely in most types of soil; drought tolerant. Once established, this species rapidly forms a weed-proof mat, particularly effective against tree seedlings. Its foliage emerges early yet remains untouched by deer. The ever popular 'Ingwersen's Variety' produces pale pink or violet flowers over light green foliage.
CHARACTERISTICS AND USE: Here is a tenacious spreader with a distinctive, aromatic foliage: its leaves are divided into seven delicately lobed segments, which turn bright yellow and red in the fall. Clusters of tiny pastel flowers appear from late spring and throughout the summer. Sometimes they'll bloom sporadically into autumn. It's a very easy plant to grow, certain to please. Its vigor may be due to its thick roots and prolific system of runners. I like to see this plant in masses, especially around the bases of trees and shrubs.

HELIOPSIS HELIANTHOIDES
Oxeye or False Sunflower
(*above*)

FAMILY: Asteraceae
NATIVE RANGE: North America
USDA ZONES: 3–9
TYPE: Herbaceous
HEIGHT: 3–5 feet
SPACING: 30 inches

CONDITIONS: Prefers full sun and well-drained soil; drought tolerant. 'Summer Sun' ('Sommersonne') reaches about three feet, blooming all summer long.
CHARACTERISTICS AND USE: A reliable, brilliant source of color all summer long. *Heliopsis* is closely related to the true sunflower, though it presents itself in a less gigantic, more compact form. By midseason it produces bright yellow, daisy-like flowers with golden disks at their centers—this truly gives the garden a jolt of radiance. The flowers look splendid against their rich green foliage, at the tops of tall stems clasping pairs of serrate leaves. Perfect for massing, in sunny meadows, and for cut-flower arrangements. I enjoy seeing it planted near *Perovskia atriplicifolia, Polygonum polymorphum* (fleece flower), *Tanacetum macrophyllum, Salvia nemorosa, Veronica* x 'Goodness Grows', and various grasses.
SEE PAGE 156

HOSTA SIEBOLDIANA
Plantain Lily

FAMILY: Liliaceae
NATIVE RANGE: Japan
USDA ZONES: 4–9
TYPE: Herbaceous
HEIGHT: 30 inches

SPACING: 24 inches
CONDITIONS: Prefers shady spots with rich, moist soils; tolerates some sun. Mulch crown with grit to avoid snail and slug damage. Flowers and foliage remain on deer's top-ten list of favorite fodder. 'Francis Williams', an ever popular variety, exhibits golden-yellow variegation along its leaf edges; 'Sum and Substance' produces the largest leaves of any *Hosta*.

CHARACTERISTICS AND USE: This plant produces the largest, most impressive leaves of any *Hosta*, and it adds great texture and interest to the shaded garden. The leaves are heart-shaped, rounded, and ridged, a handsome blue-green color with a dusting of white. In late spring its white, sometimes pale lilac, flowers emerge on tall, erect stalks, though these can get lost among the massive leaves. *Hosta*'s flower buds look a little like dwarf artichokes. This plant is prized for its foliage, and it works well either as an accent or massed.

SEE PAGE 170

HYPERICUM CALYCINUM
St.-John's-Wort

FAMILY: Hypericaceae
NATIVE RANGE: Southeastern Europe and Asia Minor
USDA ZONES: 4–9
TYPE: Herbaceous, though semi-evergreen with woody stems

HEIGHT: 12–18 inches
SPACING: 18–24 inches
CONDITIONS: Prefers sun or dappled shade; tolerates dry, sandy soil. Every few years, cut back to about six inches in early spring.

CHARACTERISTICS AND USE: This fine plant is a real trooper: it grows fast, blooms prolifically, and spreads through stolons. Wolfgang calls it "one of the best ground covers for sun or partial shade." From mid- to late summer, it produces glowing yellow flowers against rich green foliage. Blooms are composed of five petals encircling a thick tuft of stamens. *Hypericum*'s lustrous leaves turn slightly purple in the fall, and the color remains until early spring. Take Wolfgang's advice and plant it beneath deciduous trees, such as *Betula nigra*, or layer it along banks or slopes. Also plant it in association with *Panicum virgatum*, *Pennisetum alopecuroides*, and *Polygonum polymorphum* (fleece flower).

SEE PAGES 76–77

LIATRIS SPICATA
Gayfeather (*right*)

FAMILY: Compositae
NATIVE RANGE: Eastern and central United States
USDA ZONES: 5–9
TYPE: Herbaceous
HEIGHT: 24–30 inches
SPACING: 24 inches

CONDITIONS: Prefers sun or partial shade in moist, sandy soils; fairly drought tolerant; self-seeds under right conditions. 'Alba' is a white-flowering selection.

CHARACTERISTICS AND USE: This classic American native seems to be in great demand among those in the floral trade—a real signal that it has "arrived" as a popular flower. *Liatris* is wonderfully suited to the garden—it produces a brilliant violet inflorescence that attracts butterfly and human alike. Its distinctive flower spikes, which range from 6 inches to 18 inches tall, bloom from the tips down, unlike most other flowering plants. Its narrow leaves whirl around clump-forming stems and gently arch toward the ground. Plant *Liatris* in masses, in the meadow, as a vertical accent, and for use as a cut flower.

I think it's particularly dramatic when planted near *Coreopsis verticillata, Nepeta sibirica,* and *Perovskia atriplicifolia.*
SEE PAGES 24, 26 (top)

LIGULARIA DENTATA
Bigleaf Goldenray

FAMILY: Compositae
NATIVE RANGE: China
USDA ZONES: 4–9
TYPE: Herbaceous
HEIGHT: 36–42 inches
SPACING: 24 inches
CONDITIONS: Prefers partial shade as leaves will wilt with too much afternoon sun. Requires moist to boggy soils, where it readily self-seeds and colonizes. Mulch crown with grit to avoid snail and slug damage. 'Woerlitzer Gold' is one of the more recent selections on the market.
CHARACTERISTICS AND USE: Another darling of the butterflies, *Ligularia* has large, leathery, kidney-shaped leaves that show a deep green above and maroon to mahogany underneath and radiate from a central core. In late summer, its deep yellow, daisylike flowers appear on stout stalks, high above the foliage. They can almost disappear at this point beneath a cloud of monarch butterflies. I use it in masses, often along the north and east sides of buildings or walls (since it shrinks from the hot afternoon sun). It looks very fine with *Hosta* spp., *Osmunda cinnamomea* (cinnamon fern), and *Polygonum amplexicaule* 'Firetail'.

NEPETA SIBIRICA
Catmint *(below)*

FAMILY: Labiatae
NATIVE RANGE: Siberia, China
USDA ZONES: 4–9
TYPE: Herbaceous
HEIGHT: 24 inches
SPACING: 24 inches
CONDITIONS: Prefers full sun and well-drained soil; drought tolerant. After flowers fade, cut back stalks to encourage another round of blooms. To prevent cats from rolling in foliage, place thorny rose or barberry twigs around base of plant. *Nepeta* x *faassenii* (catnip) is shorter in height and blooming period than *N. sibirica.*
CHARACTERISTICS AND USE: Since it belongs in the mint family, *Nepeta* shares many mintlike characteristics, such as scented leaves paired along square stems in a loose, rambling habit. *N. sibirica* grows in attractive billows of soft, gray-green foliage at the first sign of spring. In early and midsummer, a haze of small lavender trumpet flowers blooms prolifically. Its aromatic foliage and flowers invite bees, butterflies, and, yes, the inevitable cats. Plant *Nepeta* in masses, in your herb or kitchen garden, and by all means use it in dried arrangements. I also like to see it accompany *Achillea filipendulina, Coreopsis verticillata, Liatris spicata, Perovskia atriplicifolia,* and *Tanacetum macrophyllum.*

OENOTHERA SPECIOSA
Rose Sundrop

FAMILY: Onagraceae
NATIVE RANGE: South-central North America
USDA ZONES: 5–8
TYPE: Herbaceous, though

stems are woody near base
HEIGHT: 12–18 inches
SPACING: 24 inches
CONDITIONS: Likes loose,
well-drained soils; sun loving
and drought tolerant. 'Rosea'
produces pure pink flowers.
CHARACTERISTICS AND USE:
Here is an extremely hardy
native plant that spreads freely
via rhizomes. And what a heavenly display it creates, all summer long! Bright, cup-shaped
flowers create a carpet over
mounds of gray-green foliage.
The dreamy flowers have four
petals that pale from soft pink to
white to yellow at the center.
"People can't believe their
eyes," comments Wolfgang.
Plant *Oenothera* in masses, for
naturalizing, and also use it
among stones. It looks wonderful
among *Salvia* x *superba* (sage),
Yucca filamentosa, and various
grasses.

PEROVSKIA
ATRIPLICIFOLIA
Russian Sage

FAMILY: Labiatae
NATIVE RANGE: Asia,
Afghanistan to Tibet
USDA ZONES: 5–9
TYPE: Deciduous sub-shrub
with woody stems
HEIGHT: 3–4 feet
SPACING: 24–30 inches
CONDITIONS: Likes loose,
well-drained soils; sun loving
and drought tolerant. Cut back

six inches from ground in late
winter.
CHARACTERISTICS AND USE:
Another delightful favorite.
Russian sage is a member of the
mint and sage family, and it
boasts spicy leaves, square
stems, and a soft, airy habit.
From early summer through
the fall, its terminal stems produce a blue cloud of tiny, fragrant blooms that overshadow
the finely cut, gray-green foliage underneath. Its silvery
stalks look handsome all year
long. This plant is good for
massing and for the herb garden. Try planting it in association with *Artemisia* spp.,
Coreopsis spp., *Hibiscus moscheutos*
(rose mallow), *Liatris spicata,*
Nepeta spp., and *Sedum* x
'Autumn Joy'.
SEE PAGES 96–97

PHYSOSTEGIA VIRGINIANA
False Dragonhead (*above*)

FAMILY: Lamiaceae
NATIVE RANGE: Eastern
North America
USDA ZONES: 3–9
TYPE: Herbaceous
HEIGHT: 3–4 feet
SPACING: 24–30 inches
CONDITIONS: Likes moist, fertile soils in full sun; withstands
poor drainage. 'Vivid' is a compact selection producing hot-
pink blooms.
CHARACTERISTICS AND USE:
Don't confuse this plant with another outstanding, pink-
flowering native, *Chelone lyonii*
(pink turtlehead). *P. virginiana* has
rigid square stems and erect
flower spikes. It forms in stiff
clumps and produces runners
with glossy, sharp-toothed
leaves. From late summer to fall,
its flowers, which look a little
like snapdragons, bloom along its

spires. False dragonhead is good for massing, swale planting, and lovely for cut-flower arrangements. I like it planted with *Aster tataricus* (tatarian daisy), *Euphorbia palustris* (spurge), *Helianthus angustifolius* (swamp sunflower), and *Vernonia noveboracensis* (New York ironweed).

POLYGONUM AMPLEXICAULE (ALSO PERSICARIA AMPLEXICAULIS)
Fleece Flower
⊲⊲⊳

FAMILY: Polygonaceae
NATIVE RANGE: Himalayas
USDA ZONES: 5–9
TYPE: Herbaceous, yet stems appear to be somewhat woody near their base
HEIGHT: 4 feet
SPACING: 30–36 inches
CONDITIONS: Likes moist, fertile soils in sun or partial shade; persistent once established. A noteworthy variety, 'Firetail', produces ruby flower spikes on four foot stems. *P. polymorphum*, another one of Wolfgang's more recent favorites, remains a relative unknown, both in the literature and on the market (Kurt Bluemel, Inc., in Baldwin, Maryland, is the only grower to offer this species in the U.S.). Similar in leaf and habit to *P. amplexicaule* yet favoring more sun and less moisture, *P. polymorphum* displays creamy white, *Aruncus*-like flowers from spring to fall.

CHARACTERISTICS AND USE: This *Polygonum* is not as invasive as some other varieties. It has distinct joints where leaves attach to stems and grows in bushy clumps of broad, pointed leaves. All summer and autumn, until the first hard frost, it produces pretty, lavender-like flower spikes that sway above its thin stalks. Fleece flower is a good companion for *Aster x frikartii* (hardy purple aster), *Brunnera macrophylla* (Siberian bugloss), *Hypericum calycinum,* and *Pennisetum alopecuroides.*

POLYSTICHUM ACROSTICHOIDES
Christmas Fern (*above*)
⊲⊲⊳

FAMILY: Polypodiaceae
NATIVE RANGE: Eastern United States to Canada
USDA ZONES: 3–9
TYPE: Herbaceous evergreen
HEIGHT: 24 inches
SPACING: 24 inches
CONDITIONS: Likes moist, humus-rich soils in full or partial shade; often found in the wild along rocky slopes, shielded beneath trees or by a northern exposure.

CHARACTERISTICS AND USE:
I love this fern's grit: it's a true
workhorse. Christmas fern's intricate, handsome foliage stays
green throughout the winter. It
grows in loose clumps, with new
growth via rhizomes. In spring,
its lovely silvery fronds emerge
in tight spirals that gradually and
gracefully unfold. Its cinnamon-
colored spores, which create
rows of spots on the backs of
mature fronds, ripen over the
summer. A marvelous evergreen
fern for massing around deciduous trees and shrubs, it's perfect
for the shade garden and for sup-
plying a steady supply of cut
greenery.

RUDBECKIA FULGIDA
Black-eyed Susan

FAMILY: Compositae
NATIVE RANGE: Eastern and
central United States
USDA ZONES: 3–9
TYPE: Herbaceous
HEIGHT: 24 inches

SPACING: 30 inches
CONDITIONS: Prefers full sun
and loose, fertile soils, remaining
moist rather than dry; readily
self-seeds. The German variety
'Goldsturm', selected and
named by Karl Foerster in 1933
in Potsdam, currently retains its
long-standing notoriety and popularity.
CHARACTERISTICS AND USE:
A long-standing favorite of ours,
this sturdy, hardy perennial colonizes sunlit areas from rhizomes. It produces a profusion of
handsome, dark-eyed daisy-like
flowers all summer long: their
radiant petals look particularly
fine against their deep green
leaves. *R. fulgida*'s black seed
cones hang on long after the
petals and foliage have fallen
away, creating a harvest for
birds and wildlife and a handsome feast for the eyes. Use for
massings of intense color, for
planting in sunny meadows, and
to enhance your winter garden.
They make strong cut flowers
and may be planted in association with *Asclepias tuberosa,
Calamagrostis* spp., *Kniphofia* spp.
(red-hot poker), *Pennisetum
alopecuroides,* and *Senecio aureus.*
SEE PAGES 74–75, 110

RUDBECKIA MAXIMA
Great Cone Flower (*left*)

FAMILY: Compositae
NATIVE RANGE: Southeastern
United States to Texas

USDA ZONES: 4–9
TYPE: Herbaceous
HEIGHT: 4–5 feet
SPACING: 30 inches
CONDITIONS: Prefers full or partial sun, and moist, well-drained
soils; withstands wet conditions.
Often found at the edge of pine
forests throughout the South;
flower stems remain more upright
when grown in mass.
CHARACTERISTICS AND USE:
The leaves of this plant are its
main attraction: they're broad,
elliptical, and have an outstanding, glaucous color. This is an
unusual native, with large,
black-eyed Susan flowers distinguished by their protracted central cones, which are encircled
by drooping golden petals. The
blooms appear in late summer on
tall stalks, up to five feet tall.
This creates quite an imposing,
if perplexing, sight. Some have
been known to ask, "What in
the world is it?" Use this
Rudbeckia as a stunning vertical
accent, or plant it in mass, for an
even more striking effect. It's
also fine in sunny meadows or
along the woodland edge.
SEE PAGE 64 (bottom)

SEDUM X 'AUTUMN JOY'
Stonecrop

FAMILY: Crassulaceae
NATIVE RANGE: Japan,
Europe to Siberia
USDA ZONES: 3–9
TYPE: Herbaceous

HEIGHT: 18–24 inches
SPACING: 18–24 inches
CONDITIONS: Prefers sun but
will grow in partial shade; extremely drought tolerant.
Selected in Germany and named
'Herbstfreude' (*S. spectabile* x
S. telephium). *Sedum* x 'Rudy
Glow' (*S. telephium* x *S. cauticola*)
admirably serves as a low
ground cover, especially when
planted among stepping stones.
Reaching half the height of
'Autumn Joy', 'Ruby Glow' exhibits a less rigid yet more re-
fined character: its foliage
follows gently curving stems,
taking on highlights of burgundy over the course of summer. By midsummer, flower
clusters reach their peak in an
array of iridescent reds.

CHARACTERISTICS AND USE:
This is a year-round winner: a
four-season perennial whose pale
green, broccoli-like flower buds
first emerge early in the season.
Gradually these turn the color of
salmon, finally achieving full
bloom in late summer, then
darken to crimson over the cooler
fall days. All winter, its dark

brown dried flower clusters keep
their form. And each spring,
new mounds of rosettes emerge,
which slowly develop into erect
stems of gray-green succulentlike
foliage. This is a wonderful plant
for ground cover massing and for
adding character to the winter
garden. It also looks fine planted
with *Coreopsis verticillata,
Caryopteris* x *clandonensis,
Pennisetum alopecuroides, Sesleria
autumnalis* (autumn moor grass),
and *Yucca filamentosa*.
SEE PAGE(S): 22, 28

SENECIO AUREUS
Golden Groundsel (*below*)
〰️

FAMILY: Compositae
NATIVE RANGE: Eastern and
central United States
USDA ZONES: 5–8
TYPE: Herbaceous, semi-
evergreen
HEIGHT: 18 inches
SPACING: 18 inches
CONDITIONS: Grows in sun or
shade; thrives in moist, loamy
soils; withstands wet feet; often
found naturalized in drainage
swales.

CHARACTERISTICS AND USE:
This moisture lover forms in
clumps and produces lustrous
foliage and radiant blooms.
Senecio has toothed basal
leaves that stay green through
the winter, though their back-
sides become tinged with purple. In midspring, smooth
stems shoot up, nurturing
clusters of golden daisy-like
flowers. *Senecio* also spreads
with abandon on runners
from aromatic roots. This is a
good perennial to plant in
mass. It works well as ground
cover beneath trees and shrubs
and looks lovely along the
woodland edge, in a bog garden, or in damp meadows.
Plant it in association with
Chelone lyonii (turtlehead),
Helianthus angustifolius (swamp
sunflower), and *Venonia
noveboracensis* (New York
ironweed).

SOLIDAGO RUGOSA
Goldenrod
〰️

FAMILY: Compositae
NATIVE RANGE: Eastern
United States to Canada
USDA ZONES: 3–9
TYPE: Herbaceous
HEIGHT: 5–8 feet
SPACING: 36 inches
CONDITIONS: Prefers full sun
or light shade; tolerates hot, dry
conditions. A recent selection,
'Fireworks', produces dramatic
floral displays.

CHARACTERISTICS AND USE: Here is a beautiful, hardy, rugged native flower that grows wild along roadsides and railways. Because it frequently grows near ragweed, goldenrod is often blamed—unjustly—for causing hay fever. (So, allergy sufferers: plant this perennial without fear.) *S. rugosa* forms strong clumps and produces hairy, upright stems of whorls with serrate leaves. In late summer, sprays of golden-yellow blooms cascade along its arching panicles, creating a fiery display as the weather cools. I like using goldenrod in mass as a ground cover and in meadows. I also plant it near *Aster* spp., *Eupatorium* spp. (joe-pye weed), *Rudbeckia* spp., and *Sedum* spp. SEE PAGE 95

TANACETUM MACROPHYLLUM (ALSO *CHRYSANTHEMUM MACROPHYLLUM*)
Tansy Daisy

≈≈

FAMILY: Compositae
NATIVE RANGE: Southeastern Europe to the Caucasus and Asia Minor
USDA ZONES: 5–8
TYPE: Herbaceous
HEIGHT: 4 feet
SPACING: 30 inches
CONDITIONS: Tough and resilient; will grow most anywhere in sun or partial shade; tolerates dry soils; spreads by

self-seeding. *Tanacetum* is one of Wolfgang's more recent favorites.
CHARACTERISTICS AND USE: A relative newcomer, though fast becoming one of our favorite plants, this variety has a flower and leaf that resemble *Achillea*'s. Its off-white, daisy-like flower heads appear in dense, flat clusters on the tops of tall stems by midsummer. It has a nice feathery, gray-green foliage that decorates the length of the stems, though its basal leaves are noticeably larger and denser. It's prized for its leaf, and increasingly we are recommending it as an ornamental, for massing, meadows, or the woodland edge.

TIARELLA CORDIFOLIA
Foamflower (*above*)

≈≈

FAMILY: Saxifragaceae
NATIVE RANGE: Eastern North America
USDA ZONES: 3–8
TYPE: Herbaceous, semi-evergreen
HEIGHT: 12 inches
SPACING: 18 inches
CONDITIONS: Prefers full to partial shade in humus-rich, moist soils.
CHARACTERISTICS AND USE: A lovely woodland plant, *T. cordifolia*'s fresh foliage and light, "foamy" flowers present a welcome spring sight. Its leaves are similar to those of *Heuchera* (coral bells): they're heart-shaped and serrated, with prominent veins, and they darken to burgundy and bronze in autumn. Its multitude of fine, wispy blooms

gather on long-lasting, pink-tinged flower spikes. Each resembles a tiny tiara. *T. cordifolia* spreads freely from stolons and unfolds in a carpet of green and white. A great choice for massing, it's especially beautiful as a ground cover beneath trees and shrubs, and it's perfect for the woodland garden. Plant it in association with *Chrysogonum virginianum* (green and gold), *Polygonatum* spp. (Solomon's seal), *Sanguinaria canadensis* (bloodroot), *Trillium* spp. (trillium), and various ferns.

YUCCA FILAMENTOSA
Adam's Needle *(above)*

&ℰ&

FAMILY: Agavaceae
NATIVE RANGE: Southeastern United States
USDA ZONES: 3–9
TYPE: Evergreen, somewhat woody
HEIGHT: 5–6 feet
SPACING: 30 inches

CONDITIONS: Prefers full sun in well-drained soils; extremely tolerant of drought, heat, and humidity. Wolfgang claims "it will grow anywhere," though he cautions that one not plant *Yuccas* where their pointed blades may pose a hazard to children at play.

CHARACTERISTICS AND USE: I love this dramatic, incredibly hardy native because it adds such wonderful texture and structure to the garden. Once established, *Yucca*'s here to stay: new rosettes readily regenerate from severed root stems. Swordlike leaves appear like blue-green blades dusted with gray and terminate in sharp spines. Their leaf margins shed fine, curling threads. In summer the flower stalks shoot up, appearing at first like giant asparagus and branching out to support dozens of white, nodding blooms. The flowers are particularly fragrant in the night air. Both flower pods and their stalks dry to a dark brown but retain their rigid sculptural form admirably in the face of winter's assault. *Yucca* can be used for massing or as an accent, and it's a fine choice for the winter garden. I like it planted near *Acanthus* spp., *Coreopsis* spp., *Euphorbia* spp. (spurge), *Hemerocallis* spp. (daylily), *Kniphofia* spp. (red-hot poker), *Sedum* x 'Autumn Joy', and various grasses.

SEE PAGE 27

GRASSES AND SEDGES

CALAMAGROSTIS ACUTIFLORA STRICTA
Feather Reed Grass

❧

FAMILY: Gramineae
NATIVE RANGE: Europe
USDA ZONES: 4–9
TYPE: Herbaceous
HEIGHT: 4–6 feet
SPACING: 30 inches
CONDITIONS: Prefers full or partial sun in well-drained soil; flower stalks tend to flop over in shade. Karl Foerster discovered this clump-forming variety, also known as C. x acutiflora 'Karl Foerster', along a railway in Germany: one day he pulled the emergency brake on the train he had boarded so not to miss a key opportunity for collecting stock.
CHARACTERISTICS AND USE: This hardy grass favors cool seasons and has a distinct, vertical habit. It's a stunning plant, creating year-round interest, and it is also one of the first ornamentals to leaf out in early spring, which I think makes it particularly appealing. By summertime, its erect flower stalks shoot skyward from rich clumps of fresh green blades. Its fine panicle flowers open again in the fall and later dry to the color of ripe wheat. Even the seed stems remain erect throughout the cold months, providing vivid, vertical forms in the winter garden. Select feather reed grass for massing, winter interest, and for use as a sharp, vertical accent. It looks wonderful in large planters, and I like to plant it in association with Aster spp., Pennisetum alopecuroides, Rudbeckia fulgida 'Goldsturm', and Sedum x 'Autumn Joy'.

SEE PAGE 30

CAREX MORROWII VARIEGATA
Variegated Japanese Sedge
(below)

❧

FAMILY: Cyperaceae
NATIVE RANGE: Japan
USDA ZONES: 5–9
TYPE: Herbaceous, semi-evergreen
HEIGHT: 12 inches
SPACING: 18 inches
CONDITIONS: Prefers cool shade in moist soils, yet admirably withstands heat and drought.
CHARACTERISTICS AND USE: Although not a true grass, this variety tends to prefer northern climates. It has sharp, three-edged blades that grow in a compact form and unfold in dense clumps of deep green foliage, striated with narrow silver bands that reflect the light beautifully in shaded spaces. It's great for brightening shady areas that otherwise appear too shadowed, but its flowers are insignificant. I recommend massing the plants, using them for edging and defining borders,

and planting them in association with *Bergenia cordifolia* (heartleaf bergenia), *Epimedium* spp., and *Rodgersia pinnata* (bronzeleaf Rodgersia).

CHASMANTHIUM LATIFOLIUM (FORMERLY *UNIOLA LATIFOLIA*)
Wild Oats *(below)*

FAMILY: Gramineae
NATIVE RANGE: Eastern North America
USDA ZONES: 4–8
TYPE: Herbaceous
HEIGHT: 3–4 feet
SPACING: 18 inches
CONDITIONS: Grows best in partial shade, preferring well-drained, humus-rich soil;

a prolific self-seeder. Not adaptable to seaside settings; prevails as a popular ornamental species in Europe.

CHARACTERISTICS AND USE: This lovely, warm-season grass, a true woodland species, should not be confused with the native dune grass, *Uniola paniculata* (sea oats), despite being sometimes known by the same common name. *C. latifolia* has a broad, attractive, green leaf blade, and its flat, oatlike flowers ripen to

bronze by autumn. Its seed pods remain gracefully suspended along its arching stems from the end of summer throughout the fall, and the dead foliage is straw-colored. This is a beautiful variety for cut or dried arrangements and for massing and planting at the woodland edge (I use it to create a graceful transition from forest to open meadow or lawn). Its decorative seeds are particularly fine. Try planting it close by *Anemone japonica*

(Japanese anemone), *Cimicifuga* spp., *Kirengeshoma palmata* (yatabe), and *Polygonatum* spp. (Solomon's seal).

FARGESIA NITIDA (FORMERLY SINARUNDINARIA NITIDA)
Blue Clump Bamboo
❧❧

FAMILY: Gramineae
NATIVE RANGE: China
USDA ZONES: 4–9
TYPE: Semi-evergreen with woody canes
HEIGHT: 6–8 feet
SPACING: 12–15 feet
CONDITIONS: Does best in full or partial shade with ample moisture; requires more shade in warmer climates and sheltered spots in colder regions; never needs to be cut back or pruned. *F. murielae* is a notable similar species.
CHARACTERISTICS AND USE: Wolfgang calls this plant with a clump-forming nature "a great bamboo without runners." Sometimes *F. nitida* is considered part of the genus *Arundinaria* (bamboo); fortunately, by planting it you can have the grace and interest of bamboo without being overrun by it: *F. nitida* is self-contained and noninvasive. It grows slowly and sends up new shoots rigidly above older canes, which, over time, acquire a graceful arching form, or "weeping" habit. Like other varieties of bamboo, *F. nitida* flow-

ers only about once in a hundred years. Interestingly, single species in large regions may bloom simultaneously, over the course of a year, after which most tend to die. So when you purchase your plants, take note of their blooming period—it is a rare sight. This makes a stunning presence by the water's edge because of its dramatic sculptural form. I also use it as an accent or for screening.
SEE PAGES 2, 146

HAKONECHLOA MACRA
Hakone Grass
❧❧

FAMILY: Gramineae
NATIVE RANGE: Japan
USDA ZONES: 5–9
TYPE: Herbaceous
HEIGHT: 1–2 feet
SPACING: 30 inches
CONDITIONS: Grows in sun or shade, preferring rich, moist, well-drained soils. Variegated varieties tend to be less hardy than solid-green stock.
CHARACTERISTICS AND USE: I like this elegant, cool-season grass, which grows in soft, bright green layers of foliage that arch and billow in the wind. Hakone grass is indigenous to the rugged, mountainous cliffs of Japan and creeps through rhizomes though remains noninvasive. Its autumn foliage is a handsome bronze with red highlights, similar to *Imperata cylindrica* (Japanese blood grass).

Its flowers, though, are insignificant and appear in late summer. I use it for massing—it works well as a low-growing ground cover—but I also like to see it in containers, spilling over the edges. It makes an attractive border for walkways and terraces and looks good in association with *Hosta* spp.
SEE PAGE 171

MISCANTHUS SINENSIS
Silver Grass
(page 194, bottom left)
❧❧

FAMILY: Gramineae
NATIVE RANGE: China and Japan
USDA ZONES: 4–9
TYPE: Herbaceous
HEIGHT: 3–6 feet
SPACING: 36 inches
CONDITIONS: Grows best in full sun or partial shade with average soils and sufficient moisture; tolerates dry conditions once established. Self-seeds, often escaping garden settings and taking root in the wild. Centers of mature specimens tend to die out; divide these every five to ten years to keep clumps youthful and strong. By late winter, cut dried stalks six inches from the ground. Numerous varieties exist with many more in cultivation; several of our favorites include:
M. sinensis giganteus (giant

Chinese silver grass), also named *M. floridulus,* is a robust, clump-forming giant that reaches as high as twelve feet.

M. sinensis 'Gracillimus' (Japanese maiden grass) forms dense clumps with an attractive texture.

M. sinensis 'Malepartus' (silver grass), a recent selection by Ernst Pagels, produces large flowers in early summer.

M. sinensis purpurascens (red maiden grass) remains fairly compact, its foliage turning auburn by fall; a good selection for planters.

M. sinensis 'Rotsilber' (Chinese silver grass), another recent Ernst Pagels selection, blooms earlier than most with reddish inflorescence.

CHARACTERISTICS AND USE: This is one of our mainstays. It's the ornamental grass most often chosen by Americans seeking to replace their turf lawns. *M. sinensis*'s popularity is well deserved: it forms strong clumps of delicately arching blades marked by a

ROGER FOLEY

ROGER FOLEY

white stripe at midrib. In late summer, silky flowers rise high above the leaves, and as downy seeds develop, its flower panicles curl gently—they have a soft, feathery quality. Flowers and foliage dry to a warm straw color and stand tall through fall and winter. Try using it as an accent, for screening at eye level, in cut- or dried-flower arrangements, and planted alongside *Aster* spp., *Pennisetum* spp., *Rudbeckia* spp.,

and *Sedum* spp. A cautionary note: although *M. sinensis* produces a strong, reliable showing throughout the year, plant it sparingly, because it likes to spread beyond the garden's confines.
SEE PAGES 49, 76–77

MOLINIA CAERULEA ARUNDINACEA
Tall Purple Moor Grass (*above*)

FAMILY: Gramineae
NATIVE RANGE: Europe, Asia
USDA ZONES: 3–8
TYPE: Herbaceous
HEIGHT: 6–8 feet
SPACING: 36–42 inches
CONDITIONS: Grows best in full sun with acidic, humus-rich soils and sufficient moisture. 'Windspiel', selected by Karl Foerster, is prized for its height and vigorous growth.
CHARACTERISTICS AND USE: This is an exquisite plant, a consummate garden ornamental whose subtle colors and refine-

FAMILY: Gramineae

NATIVE RANGE: Northeastern to central North America

USDA ZONES: 3–9

TYPE: Herbaceous

HEIGHT: 3–4 feet

SPACING: 30 inches

CONDITIONS: Grows best in full sun with rich, moist soils, yet tolerates drought and average soils. Recent selections include 'Cloud Nine', the tallest variety currently available; 'Haense Herms', offering reddish brown fall foliage; and 'Heavy Metal', with its upright, metallic blue blades.

CHARACTERISTICS AND USE: A true American prairie grass. Happily, it also works well in most domesticated gardens too. Its lush foliage and its lovely haze of flowers are perfect backdrops for colorful perennials. By late summer, airy pink spikes seem to float over its dense clumps of brilliant green foliage. Autumn turns both foliage and flowers yellow and brown; the muted colors soften the stark winter landscape. Use this plant for massing in borders or meadows, along the woodland edge, and in planters so that it cascades over the rims. I think switch grass is a perfect complement to *Aster* spp., *Boltonia asteroides*, *Sedum* spp., and *Yucca filamentosa*.

SEE PAGE 95

ment belies its wild native origins among the peat bogs and heather-covered moors of Europe. From tufts of ribbony foliage, fine flower stalks shoot up, sometimes growing to a height of three feet or more. The stalks support wisps of purple flower heads on nearly transparent, delicate stems, which sway and rustle in the breeze. Autumn seeds turn gold to match the mounds of foliage underneath. I love this grass's elegant display of color and movement. I recommend planting it as a specimen; for a kinetic, vertical accent; as a screen for filtering light; and in cut- or dried-flower arrangements. A fine choice to plant near *Coreopsis* spp. and *Sedum* spp.

SEE PAGE 65

ROGER FOLEY

PENNISETUM ALOPECUROIDES

Fountain Grass (*above*)

⊰☙☙

FAMILY: Gramineae
NATIVE RANGE: Eastern Asia
USDA ZONES: 4–9
TYPE: Herbaceous
HEIGHT: 2–4 feet
SPACING: 30 inches
CONDITIONS: Prefers sun or partial shade in moist, fertile soils; likes damp conditions, with a tendency to self-seed. Many interesting varieties are available, like 'Moudry', with its dark foliage and inflorescence.
CHARACTERISTICS AND USE: Here is another of my favorites, a reliable, graceful ornamental grass resembling a fountain with arching jets of water radiating from a center point. All summer long its flower stems display handsome foxtail plumes that emulate its leaf blades. At their peak the blooms sparkle with silver and red highlights that glint in the sun or when laced with dew. Both foliage and seed heads dry to a pleasant golden tan that lasts well into winter. Use it for massing or bordering the edge of a pool (it spills evocatively over coping stones) and plant it near *Aster* spp., *Eupatorium* spp. (joe-pye weed), *Rudbeckia* spp., *Sedum* spp., and *Yucca filamentosa*.
SEE PAGE 132

SORGHASTRUM NUTANS

Indian Grass (*opposite left*)

⊰☙☙

FAMILY: Gramineae
NATIVE RANGE: Eastern and central North America
USDA ZONES: 4–9
TYPE: Herbaceous
HEIGHT: 4–6 feet
SPACING: 30 inches
CONDITIONS: Hardy and drought resistant, preferring full sun in well-drained, loamy soils; 'Sioux Blue' is a popular selection, with blue blades in an upright habit; Kurt Bluemel, Inc., in Baldwin, Maryland, is always sold out.
CHARACTERISTICS AND USE: This is an outstanding native grass whose hardiness rivals that of *Andropogon* spp. (broom-sedge and bluestem), two other indigenous species famous for their tenacity. This variety forms strong clumps, like sorghum. It produces stiff gray-green blades that tend to bend to the earth at their tips. Midsummer brings out its beautiful, russet plumes on four-foot stems that arch in the wind. Autumn burnishes its foliage and seed heads to a deep gold that lasts into winter. Use it for massing, as an accent, scattered through open meadows, or for a filtered screen. This plant looks wonderful with so many others: I like to plant it near *Asclepias tuberosa*, *Aster* spp., *Dodecatheon meadia* (shooting star), *Echinacea purpurea*,

drought tolerant; prefers sun or partial shade in moist, fertile soils; slow to establish, creeping via rhizomes.

CHARACTERISTICS AND USE: Wolfgang claims *S. sibiricus* is his "absolute favorite" ornamental grass. He loves its vigor and the way it thrives under so many diverse garden conditions. As a cool-season grass, its lush, bamboo-like foliage is unexpected. By midsummer, upright flower spikes emerge, supporting a luminous inflorescence. The blooms seem to glow when backlit. Autumn opens the spikes again with ripened seeds. Its leaves turn from golden yellow to a deep wine-red, though they die out after the first hard frost. Use it for massing, as an accent, or for a filtered screen. It looks particularly well in walled gardens and planted near *Aster* spp., *Hemerocallis* spp. (daylily), *Rudbeckia* spp., *Sedum* spp., and *Stachys* spp. (lamb's ears).

SEE PAGES 74–75

Filipendula rubra (queen of the prairie), *Geum triflorum* (prairie smoke), *Helianthus* spp. (sunflower), *Heliopsis* spp. (oxeye), *Liatris* spp., *Ratibida pinnata* (yellow coneflower), *Rudbeckia* spp., *Penstemon* spp. (beard tongue), and other sun-loving prairie species.

SPODIOPOGON SIBIRICUS

Silver Spike Grass (*right*)

FAMILY: Gramineae
NATIVE RANGE: Siberia to North China, Korea, and Japan
USDA ZONES: 3–9
TYPE: Herbaceous
HEIGHT: 3–5 feet
SPACING: 30 inches
CONDITIONS: Hardy and

VINES

CAMPSIS RADICANS
American Trumpet Creeper

FAMILY: Bignoniaceae
NATIVE RANGE: Eastern
United States to Texas
USDA ZONES: 4–9
TYPE: Deciduous
HEIGHT: 30–40 feet
CONDITIONS: Grows in any
type of soil; withstands heat,
sun, drought, and urban condi-
tions. Prune regularly to keep in
check and stimulate flowering.
CHARACTERISTICS AND USE:
This rampant, late-leafing native
vine is notorious for its tenacious

habit and vigorous growth, particularly in the South. It clings
to surfaces with rootlike hold-
fasts or, in the absence of support, runs freely along the
ground. All summer long its
fiery trumpet-shaped flowers
adorn stems in intense oranges
and reds, inviting swarms of
hummingbirds with its scent
and dazzling display. Like
Yucca filamentosa, *C. radicans*
produces suckers from root
pieces: once established, it's
there to stay. I use it on arbors
or trellises, for rock-pile cover,
and along fences and posts; but
beware, use it sparingly: a
little trumpet vine goes a
long way.

CLEMATIS PANICULATA
(ALSO CLEMATIS MAXIMOWIZCIANA)
Sweet Autumn Clematis (*left*)

FAMILY: Ranunculaceae
NATIVE RANGE: Japan
USDA ZONES: 3–8
TYPE: Deciduous
HEIGHT: 30–40 feet
CONDITIONS: Prefers partial
shade in moist, well-drained
soil; requires continuous mois-
ture in full sun; self-seeds.
CHARACTERISTICS AND USE:
This profuse bloomer is a vigor-
ous climber and twines around
trellises and arbors with ten-

drils. It greatly resembles its
earlier-blooming cousin, *C. virginiana* (virgin's bower clematis)
in its habit, foliage, and flower.
I like this particularly prolific
variety: by summer's end, its
vines are draped in bouquets of
fragrant white flowers fit for a
bride. In autumn as petals drop,
its downy, silvery seeds develop
and remain throughout the season. This is another good choice
for arbors, trellises, stone walls,
rock outcroppings, and fences
and posts.
SEE PAGE 120

HYDRANGEA ANOMALA PETIOLARIS
Climbing Hydrangea (*below*)

FAMILY: Hydrangeaceae
NATIVE RANGE: Himalayas,
China, Japan
USDA ZONES: 4–7
TYPE: Deciduous
HEIGHT: 60–80 feet

CONDITIONS: Prefers fertile, moist, well-drained soil in partial shade; tolerates salt air; fast growing once established. A good candidate for shade.

CHARACTERISTICS AND USE: Here is a good, hardy woody vine that develops thick stems (similar to *Parthenocissus quinquefolia*, or Virginia creeper). Its mature wood exfoliates to a handsome cinnamon-brown color, and its shiny dark green foliage easily covers walls, tree trunks, fences, and grounded surfaces. I think it's the ideal substitute for *Hedera* spp. (ivy). Best of all, in early summer the vine produces masses of creamy white hydrangea flowers that are long-lasting and have a sweet fragrance; in autumn they become faintly rust-colored. Climbing hydrangea is perfect for arbors and trellises, retaining walls and rockeries, and for use as ground cover. Choose it for its seasonal interest. It also climbs trees!

LONICERA SEMPER VIRENS
Coral Honeysuckle (*below*)

FAMILY: Caprifoliaceae
NATIVE RANGE: Eastern United States to Texas
USDA ZONES: 4–8
TYPE: Deciduous
HEIGHT: 10–20 feet
CONDITIONS: Likes full sun in moist, well-drained soil; tolerates but seldom flowers in full shade. Selections of various flower colors may be found on the market. *L. periclymenum* (woodbine) produces fragrant flowers.

CHARACTERISTICS AND USE: I prefer the restrained elegance of this variety to the unruly, aggressive character of its Japanese counterpart, the highly invasive (though, to be sure, heady-scented) *L. japonica* (Japanese honeysuckle). By the end of spring,

L. sempervirens produces lovely coral blooms in clusters of drooping trumpets and attracts parties of hummingbirds, despite their lack of fragrance. In autumn it develops round red berries, which last throughout the winter. Another pleasant feature: *L. sempervirens* leafs out in early spring, and its new leafy growth is distinctly cupped and tinged with red. This is a pretty vine for arbors, trellises, lattices, porch posts, picket fences, and railings.

POLYGONUM AUBERTII

Silver Fleece Vine (*above*)

FAMILY: Polygonaceae
NATIVE RANGE: Western China
USDA ZONES: 4–8
TYPE: Deciduous
HEIGHT: 25–35 feet
CONDITIONS: Likes sun or partial shade with ample moisture, tolerating a wide range of soil conditions; readily adapts to city conditions.
CHARACTERISTICS AND USE: Wolfgang describes *P. aubertii* as a "castle cover" in reference to its rapid growth, which has been known to scale castle walls more vigorously throughout his homeland than any medieval predecessor. From midsummer to the first frost, its fragrant white flowers, often tinged with pink, cascade brilliantly over its bright green foliage. Its fleece flower adds a touch of filigree to otherwise stark geometric structures. This vine accomplishes a lot in one season: it can grow up to ten or fifteen feet a year and works well over arbors, trellises, fences, rockeries, or climbing walls, appearing well established in no time.

SELECTED
REFERENCES

Armitage, Allan M. *Herbaceous Perennial Plants*. Athens, GA: Varsity Press, Inc., 1989.

Bijhouwer, Dr. Ir. J.T.P. *Het Nederlandse Landschap*. Amsterdam: Kosmos Amsterdam Antwerpen, 1971.

————. *Nederlandsche Tuinen en Buitenplaatsen*. Amsterdam: Allert de Lange, 1946.

————. *Waarnemen en Ontwerpen in Tuin en Landschap*. Amsterdam: N.V. Uitgeverij «Argus», 1954.

Brookes, John. *The Book of Garden Design*. New York: Macmillan Publishing Company, 1991.

Brown, Emily. *Landscaping with Perennials*. Portland, OR: Timber Press, Inc., 1986.

Chatto, Beth. *The Green Tapestry*. New York: Simon & Schuster, Inc., 1989.

Church, Thomas D., Grace Hall, and Michael Laurie. *Gardens Are for People*. New York: McGraw-Hill Book Company, 1983.

Clausen, Ruth Rogers, and Nicolas H. Ekstrom. *Perennials for American Gardens*. New York: Random House, Inc., 1989.

Crowe, Sylvia. *Garden Design*. West Sussex & London: Packard Publishing Ltd. in association with Thomas Gibson Publishing, Ltd., 1981.

Dirr, Michael A. *Manual of Wood Landscape Plants*. Champaign, IL: Stipes Publishing Company, 1975.

Druse, Ken. *The Natural Garden*. New York: Clarkson N. Potter, Inc., 1989.

Elderfield, John. *Frankenthaler*. New York: Harry N. Abrams, Inc., 1989.

Faulkner, Ray, Edwin Ziegfeld, and Gerald Hill. *Art Today*. New York: Henry Holt and Company, Inc., 1953.

Frederick, Jr., William H. *The Exuberant Garden*. Boston: Little, Brown and Company, 1992.

Goodman, Cynthia. *Hans Hofmann*. Munich: Prestel-Verlag, 1990.

Grese, Robert E. *Jens Jensen*. Baltimore: The Johns Hopkins University Press, 1992.

Grounds, Roger. *Ornamental Grasses*. London: Christopher Helm, Ltd. in association with the Hardy Plant Society, 1989.

Heriteau, Jacqueline, with Dr. H. Marc Cathey. *The National Arboretum Book of Outstanding Garden Plants*. New York: Simon & Schuster, Inc., 1990.

Hobhouse, Penelope, and Elvin McDonald. *Gardens of the World*. New York: Macmillan Publishing Company, 1991.

Hortus Third. The Staff of the Liberty Hyde Bailey Hortorium. New York: Macmillan Publishing Company, 1976.

Jelitto, Leo, and Wilhelm Schacht. *Hardy Herbaceous Perennials*. Volume I, *A–K* and Volume II, *L–Z*. Portland, OR: Timber Press, Inc., 1990.

Jellicoe, Geoffrey, Susan Jellicoe, Patrick Goode, and Michael Lancaster. *The Oxford Companion to Gardens*. Oxford: Oxford University Press, 1986.

King, Peter, Carole Ottesen, and Graham Rose. *Gardening with Style*. London: Bloomsbury Publishing Ltd., 1988.

Masson, Georgina. *Italian Gardens*. New York: Harry N. Abrams, Inc., 1961.

Mosser, Monique, and Georges Teyssot. *The Architecture of Western Gardens*. Cambridge, MA: The MIT Press, 1990.

Nichols, Frederick Doveton, and Ralph E. Griswold. *Thomas Jefferson: Landscape Architect*. Charlottesville: University Press of Virginia, 1978.

Oehme, Wolfgang, James van Sweden, and Susan Rademacher Frey. *Bold Romantic Gardens*. Reston, VA: Acropolis Books, Ltd., 1990.

Ottesen, Carole. *Ornamental Grasses*. New York: McGraw-Hill Publishing Company, 1989.

Plumptre, George. *Great Gardens, Great Designers*. London: Ward Lock, 1994.

————. *The Garden Makers*. New York: Random House, Inc., 1993.

Rubin, William. *Frank Stella, 1970–1987*. New York: The Museum of Modern Art, 1987.

Strand, Mark. *Hopper*. Hopewell, NJ: Ecco Press, 1994.

Thomas, Graham Stuart. *Perennial Garden Plants*. Portland, OR: Sagapress, Inc./Timber Press, Inc., 1990.

van Sweden, James. *Gardening with Water*. New York: Random House, Inc., 1995.

Verey, Rosemary. *Rosemary Verey's Good Planting Plans*. London: Little, Brown and Company, 1993.

Woods, Christopher. *Encyclopedia of Perennials*. New York: Facts on File, Inc., 1992.

CREDITS

PHOTOGRAPHERS
James van Sweden unless otherwise noted

DESIGN PARTICIPANTS WITH OEHME AND VAN SWEDEN

THE BLUMER-MARTIN GARDEN
Rosenblum/Harb Architects

THE DIAMOND GARDEN
Shope Reno Wharton Associates, architects
Joel Shipiro, Sculptor

THE FELDMAN GARDEN
Soloman+Bauer Architects

FRANCIS SCOTT KEY PARK
Betty Mailhouse Dunston, sculptor

THE HAMOWY GARDEN
Christopher Lethbridge, architect (pool house)

INTERNATIONAL CHANCERY CENTER
Edward D. Stone, Jr., & Associates, planners
MMM Design Group, engineers

THE JACOBS GARDEN
Lester Collins, landscape architect

THE MARSH ESTATE GARDEN
Centerbrook, architects
Andrews, Miller & Associates, Inc., engineers

THE MR. AND MRS. ULRICH MEYER GARDEN
Michael J. Pado, architect

NEW AMERICAN AND FRIENDSHIP GARDENS
AT THE NATIONAL ARBORETUM
Christopher Lethbridge, architect (gazebo)
John Cavanaugh, Beverly Pepper, sculptors

PARADISE MANOR APARTMENTS
Sorg Associates, architects

THE RICHARD AND CAROLE RIFKIND GARDEN
Walzworkinc., designers

NELSON A. ROCKEFELLER PARK
Carr, Lynch, Hack & Sandell, architects
Johansson & Walcavage, landscape architects (playground)
Tom Otterness, Demetri Porphyrios, sculptors

THE CAROLE AND ALEX ROSENBERG TERRACE
Andrée Putman, interior designer
David Jacobs, Henry Moore, sculptors

WASHINGTON NATIONAL AIRPORT SOUTH PARKING GARAGE
Hartman-Cox Architects
Howard Needles Tammen & Bergendoff, engineers

INDEX

ABOUT THE AUTHOR

A Fellow of the American Society of Landscape Architects, JAMES VAN SWEDEN was trained in the United States and the Netherlands. He entered a partnership with horticulturist and landscape architect Wolfgang Oehme in 1977 and together they have been credited with creating the New American Garden style. Members of the winning design team in a recent national competition, Oehme and van Sweden will design the landscaping for the new World War II Memorial in Washington, D.C. Van Sweden was awarded the Thomas Roland Gold Medal by the Massachusetts Horticultural Society in 1987, and the Landscape Design Award by the American Horticultural Society in 1992. His first book, *Bold Romantic Gardens: The New World Landscapes of Oehme and van Sweden*, received two Awards for Excellence from the Garden Writers Association of America. *Gardening with Water* was selected by the American Horticultural Society as one of the seventy-five best books of the last seventy-five years.

ABOUT THE TYPE

THIS BOOK WAS SET IN GOUDY VILLAGE NUMBER 2, A TYPE-FACE DESIGNED BY FREDERIC WILLIAM GOUDY (1865–1947). GOUDY BEGAN HIS CAREER AS A BOOKKEEPER, BUT DEVOTED THE REST OF HIS LIFE TO THE PURSUIT OF "RECOGNIZED QUALITY" IN A PRINTING TYPE. GOUDY VILLAGE NUMBER 2 WAS PRODUCED IN 1932, AND ALTHOUGH IT IS BASED ON THE TYPES OF JENSEN IT BEARS A RESEMBLANCE TO THE FAMOUS GOUDY OLD STYLE.